RobotBASIC Projects
For Beginners

Learn to program through a fun-filled exploration of
computer graphics, robotics, physics, mathematics,
animation, and simulation.

John Blankenship
Samuel Mishal

First Edition
June 2008

Contents At A Glance

Table Of Contents

Preface

Most introductory programming classes today bore the student with problems and examples that are inappropriate for anyone new to programming. In most cases, the examples and applications studied are far from exciting because they don't address real-world situations. Instead, students are shown how to count the number of words in a sentence or find the factorial of a number. While these are things a programmer might eventually want to do, they are hardly subjects that will excite someone new to programming.

Unfortunately, even when teachers try to introduce something exciting in the classroom, they often find many obstacles. Most modern languages, for example, require the student to learn about classes or components, as well as a cryptic syntax, before *anything* (let alone something meaningful) can be accomplished. This means that most students fail to understand even basic programming concepts because they are too busy trying to cope with the idiosyncrasies of the language itself.

RobotBASIC addresses most of these problems. It is a powerful, yet extremely easy-to-use language available for any Window's based PC. In addition to all the commands you expect in any language, it has many features that make it easy to address interesting and motivational applications even for people new to programming. We are convinced of its potential as an educational tool and want to make it available to everyone. You can download your free copy from:

www.RobotBASIC.com

This book will use RobotBASIC to explore exciting subjects while you learn about programming. You will control a simulated robot, explore the geometry of computer graphics, use animation to analyze the physics of gravity, and even write a simple yet enjoyable video game.

No knowledge of programming is required. This book will start slowly, giving you everything you need before moving on to more complex topics. This does not mean that you won't have to study. Programming requires logical thinking and problem-solving skills that take time and practice to develop.

Fortunately, while learning how to program in this book you will have fun exploring interesting ideas and relevant applications.

Chapter 1

What is a Program?

A program is simply a set of instructions that allows you to tell a computer what to do. It is not unlike the instructions you would create to tell a person what to do.

Suppose you wanted to tell a person how to get to your house. You would give them a step-by-step set of instructions explaining what to do first, what to do next, and so on. A simple computer program is the same.

1.1 Computer Languages

You can write the instructions on how to get to your house in any language. You might use French or German, for example, instead of English. If you want the person to be able to follow the directions you must use a language they understand. The same applies for a computer program.

The internal design of a computer dictates the languages that it can understand. Simple computers, such as the type found in microwave ovens, generally have to be told what to do using cryptic and obscure languages that resemble shorthand. This is necessary because small computers often have limited power and minimal memory.

Today's typical PC, on the other hand, has a huge amount of memory and thousands of times the power of the computers used to put the first men on the moon. Because of this versatility, there have been many languages written for the PC. This book will use a language called RobotBASIC.

1.2 RobotBASIC

RobotBASIC is a very powerful language, yet easy to learn. It has all the mathematical capabilities you would expect from any computer language, and even a few seldom found in other systems. It also has many features that make it easy to create exciting simulations and enjoyable video games. It even has an integrated robot simulator that makes it easy to learn how to program a mobile robot.

One of the best things about RobotBASIC is that it is very easy to use. Another advantage is that it is totally FREE. RobotBASIC is a language that is powerful enough to handle complex problems and yet easy to learn and fun to use. You can download your FREE copy of RobotBASIC by visiting the web site:

www.RobotBASIC.com

Note: We suggest you download the ZIP file created especially for this book. There are other zip files with many demo programs and files for other books. After you learn the fundamentals about programming with RobotBASIC from this book, you can download some of the other zip files and study all the example programs provided in them.

Note: The web site provides information for installing everything on your computer so you will be ready to start creating programs.

When you first run RobotBASIC, you will see the screen shown in Figure 1.1. View and accept the license agreement, which basically says that you can freely use the program and give it to your friends, but you cannot sell it.

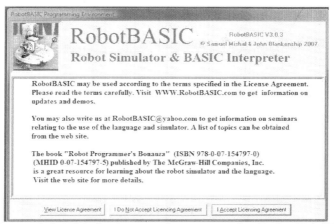

Figure 1.1: This is the opening screen for RobotBASIC

Figure 1.2: When you see this screen you are ready to program.

When you accept the license, you will get the screen shown in Figure 1.2. Some *comments* are highlighted. They show you where you will type the programs you write. Since these comments are highlighted, the first key you type will replace them. They can also be erased using the **BACKSPACE** key if you wish.

1.3 The Output or Terminal Screen

The output screen for RobotBASIC is composed of tiny dots called pixels. RobotBASIC allows you to create graphics on the screen by changing the colors of these pixels. In order to understand the graphics, you need to know how the pixels are organized.

The size of the screen is 800 pixels wide and 600 pixels tall. The pixels are numbered both horizontally and vertically starting with the number zero. Each pixel is defined by two numbers called *coordinates* that specify its position on the screen. The first number specifies the horizontal position (often referred to as the X-coordinate) and the second specifies the vertical position (the Y-coordinate).

A pixel at position 100,200 for example, would be positioned 100 pixels from the left side of the screen and 200 pixels down from the top. The pixel at position 0,0 is at the upper left corner of the screen while the coordinates 799,599 refer to the bottom right corner.

1.4 Drawing Lines

RobotBASIC allows you to draw a line on the screen using the `Line` command, which requires you to specify the starting and ending coordinates. The example below will draw a line from the upper-left corner of the screen to the lower-right corner. Notice how the coordinates 0,0 and 799,599 are entered.

```
Line 0,0,799,599
```

1.5 Running Programs

In order to see the line actually draw on the screen, we must tell RobotBASIC to run the program. We can do that in several ways. The easiest way is by clicking the  button (the green triangle) at the top of the screen. You could also use the mouse and click the RUN menu item at the top of the screen and then click the first option (Run Program). If you look carefully at that menu item, you will see it gives you a short cut option (*Ctrl-R*). This means you can also run a program by holding down the *Ctrl* key and pressing the letter R (or r).

Many actions in RobotBASIC can be achieved in a variety of ways. In the future, we will only point out one easy method for doing things. Refer to RobotBASIC's help files (by clicking the  button at the top of the editor screen) to get further information.

If you enter and run the one-line program just discussed, you will get the screen shown in Figure 1.3. Notice the line is drawn from the upper-left corner (coordinates 0,0) to the lower-right corner (coordinates 799,599).

Figure 1.3: A line drawn between two corners.

Now that you know how to enter and run a program, let's create something slightly more interesting. Click the  in

the top right corner of the output (terminal) screen to close
it (returning you to the editor screen), and then type in the
lines shown in Figure 1.4 (notice our original line is
included in the new program. Notice how some letters
have been capitalized to make reading easier. The
capitalization in this example program is not required, but it
is recommended.

```
SetColor RED
LineWidth 3
Line 0,0,799,599
SetColor Green
LineWidth 20
Line 799,0,100,500
End
```

Figure 1.4: This program draws two colorful lines.

Let's examine the program in Figure 1.4. Each line is
executed in turn starting at the beginning and continuing to
the last line. The first line sets the color used for drawing
to RED. The next line establishes how many pixels wide
the drawn lines should be. This means that the line drawn
from 0,0 to 799,599 will be red and 3 pixels wide.

The next two lines in the program set the color to green
and the width to 10. Notice that these actions only affect
future lines drawn, not any lines that have already been
drawn. This means the next line in the program draws a
wide green line from the upper-right corner of the screen
(799,0) to a position near the lower-left corner. The end
point (100,500) is positioned 100 pixels from the left and
500 pixels from the top. Run the program to see the results.

Notice the last line in the program is an END statement.
It tells the program to quit. In this particular case, the
program will stop even if you did not have an END because
there are no more lines to execute. If you add lines after
the END statement, they will not execute.

1.6 Saving and Retrieving Programs

You can save your programs at any time using the SAVE option in the FILE menu. This allows you retrieve the program later using the OPEN option. You should get into the habit of saving your programs often and definitely before you run them. This will ensure that you do not lose all your hard work if the computer crashes for some reason.

1.7 Errors in a Program

If you make a typing mistake in a program the computer may not be able to understand what you want it to do. When you run a program that has errors of any kind, RobotBASIC will alert you with an error message. If in the fifth line of Figure 1.4, for example, you wrongly spell LineWidth as LinWidth then running the program will create the error shown in Figure 1.5.

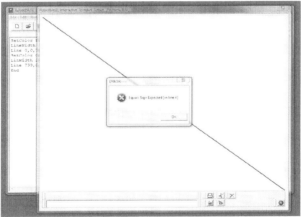

Figure 1.5: RobotBASIC tells you when it finds an error.

Notice that the program drew the red line, since the error did not occur until after that point in the program. The error message in this case (**Equals Sign Expected**) will mean more to you later in the book. At this point, all your errors are most likely caused by simple typos.

Notice also that the message tells you that the error is in Line 4 (and not Line 5 as you might expect). This is because RobotBASIC starts numbering the lines with Line 0. If you press the *OK* button, you will be returned to the editor screen and the line containing the error will be highlighted to help you find the problem. As we proceed through the book, we will examine errors and how to find them in more detail.

1.8 Adding to the Program

Suppose we want to draw a line from the center of the screen horizontally to the right edge of the screen. The center of the screen should be at 400,300 because the entire screen is 800 wide and 600 tall. If we want the ending point to be the right edge of the screen, then the X-coordinate should be 799 and the Y-coordinate needs to be the same as the Y-coordinate for the starting point, or 300 (to ensure that the line is horizontal). Add the following line just before the END statement in Figure 1.4 and run the program again. Can you predict what color the line will be? Can you change the line so it is 5 pixels wide and BLUE?

```
Line 400,300,799,300
```

> ✎ **Note:** For more colors, refer to the CONSTANTS page of the help files.

1.9 Connecting Lines (the easy way)

In addition to the Line command, RobotBASIC also has a LineTo command. The LineTo command requires only one set of coordinates, and draws a line to that point from the last point plotted. The lines below, for example, will draw a triangle. The first line draws one side. The second line continues drawing to a new point and finally, the last line draws back to the beginning point. Create a program with these lines and verify that it draws a triangle.

```
Line 200,200,300,200
LineTo 300,400
LineTo 200,200
```

Before we move on, let's test your knowledge of the material covered so far. Your goal is to write a program that will draw the triangle and the rectangle shown in Figure 1.6. The figure shows the distances (in pixels) to various sides and points of the objects. Try to write a program to draw these shapes before looking at the answer in Appendix A.

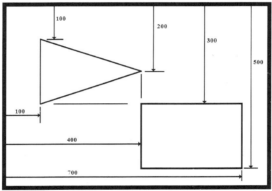

Figure 1.6: Use this information to determine the coordinates of each point of the objects.

1.10 The Robot Simulator

Now that you have some background in screen coordinates, let's see how we can create a robot and move it around on the screen. The robot simulator in RobotBASIC creates a robot using the rLocate command. The following line will create a robot at coordinates 100,200.

```
rLocate 100,200
```

Enter the above line as a single line program and run it. You will see a screen with a small circular robot in the upper-left corner. The line inside the circle indicates the direction the robot is facing (the default direction is up).

Enter the program shown in Figure 1.7. It demonstrates how to create a robot, tell it to turn right 90° and then move forward 500 pixels, turn around, and go back to its original position. Run the program and verify that it does what is expected.

```
rLocate 100,200
rTurn 90
rForward 500
rTurn 180
rForward 500
End
```

Figure 1.7: This program moves a robot on the screen.

There are several things to notice in Figure 1.7. All the commands that relate to the robot in RobotBASIC start with the letter 'r'. Notice also that some letters in commands are capitalized. This is only done for readability. The commands in RobotBASIC are *not* case-sensitive.

The rForward command moves the robot forward a specified number of pixels (or backwards if you use a negative number for the distance to be moved). The rTurn command turns the robot clockwise the specified number of degrees (or counter-clockwise if the *argument* is negative).

If the robot moves too fast on your computer you can slow it down by inserting the following line immediately after the rLocate command.

rSpeed 10

The *argument* (a parameter given to a command , 10 in this example) in the rSpeed command determines how fast the robot moves. The larger the number the slower the movement, the default number 0 produces the fastest speed. In some situations it may be an advantage to slow down the robot in order to see what actions it is taking, but usually we will want the robot to move as fast as it can. Try adding two rSpeed commands to Figure 1.6 to cause the robot to move from left to right slowly, but then move very fast as it travels back to its original position. If you have trouble, refer to the answers in Appendix A.

1.11 Summary

In this chapter, you have learned:

- ❑ About the coordinate system used by RobotBASIC.
- ❑ How to enter and run a RobotBASIC program.
- ❑ How to draw shapes using lines of different colors and different widths.
- ❑ How to create and move the simulated robot at different speeds.

1.12 Exercises

Before moving on to the next chapter, test your knowledge and skill by trying the following exercises. Give each problem your best effort before reviewing the answers given in Appendix A.

1. Create a robot in the upper-left corner of the screen and make the robot move around the perimeter of the screen (in a rectangular motion) until it gets back to its original position.

> ✎ **Note:** If you move the robot so that it hits a wall, it will cause an error. This situation will be addressed in a later chapter.

2. Create a robot in the upper-left corner of the screen and make the robot move diagonally down to the lower-right corner and then back to its original position.

Note: The RobotBASIC ZIP file you downloaded contains some of the larger programs in this book already typed for you. In most cases though, you will have to type the programs yourself - don't worry, most are short. Forcing you to type the programs is intentional. We have taught programming to many students, and we know you will learn more and learn faster if you become fully involved with the programming process. Trust us! The results will be worth the extra efforts you are about to face.

Chapter 2

Variables

In Chapter 1 you were introduced to programming. In this chapter you will learn about variables and how they help in writing more sophisticated programs.

2.1 What is a Variable?

A variable is an area in the memory of the computer that is given a name. This area can store a number (or text) whose value can be changed during the progress of a program. This is why it is called a variable. If you have studied Algebra you know that you can use variables in formulas to do calculations. Computer programs can do the same thing with programming variables.

For example, if we are talking about a rectangle it might have a width of 200 and a height of 100, but these numbers refer to one specific rectangle. Often in programming, we would like to write *code* (programming statements) that refers to a generalized situation. For example, we might want our program to draw rectangles and refer to the size of the rectangle using the variables called **width** and **height**.

2.2 Case Sensitivity

Unlike commands, the variables in RobotBASIC *are* case sensitive. This means that **width**, **Width**, and **WIDTH** are all *different* variables. This can be advantageous, but it also means you must be careful not to make typographical errors.

Variables are often meaningful words (like **width**) but they can also be just a single letter (like **A** or **x**). The variables in RobotBASIC can hold numbers (like 6 and 92.3) and words (like "hello"). For now, we will only be using numbers. We assign values to a variable using the = sign. We can also perform calculations using variables. Figure 2.1 shows a program to help clarify these ideas.

```
cat = 6
dog = 4
bird = cat*3 + dog
print cat
cat = cat * dog
Print cat
Print dog
Print bird
End
```

Figure 2.1: This program demonstrates variables.

If you run the program in Figure 2.1, it will print four numbers (6, 24, 4, and 22). Let's see how that happens. When the program starts, the variable **cat** is assigned a value of 6 and **dog** is assigned 4.

In the next line, **cat** is multiplied by 3 (forming 18) and added to **dog** (forming 22), which is stored in the variable **bird**. The next line multiplies the current value of **cat** (6) and **dog** to form 24. That value is stored back into **cat** (overwriting the previous value of 6).

The Print statements print the values of the variables specified as arguments. Notice that **cat** is printed twice so you can see that its value changes. The first Print statement will print at the top of the screen and each subsequent Print will print on the next line down. There are other options for Print as well as other commands for printing. We will discuss other options when they are needed, or you can refer to the RobotBASIC HELP files for more information.

> ✍ **Note:** RobotBASIC will issue an error if you try to use a variable as part of a calculation before you have assigned it a value.

2.3 Rectangles

Let's try an example that demonstrates the graphic command, `rectangle`. You have to give it four *arguments*. The first two represent the coordinates of the upper-left corner and the last two, the lower-right corner of the rectangle to be drawn. As an example, the line of code below will draw a rectangle whose upper-left corner is 50,100 and the lower-right corner is 500,250. Notice the width of this rectangle is 450 and its height is 150 (the width is the difference between the two X-coordinates and the height is the difference between the two Y-coordinates).

```
Rectangle 50, 100, 500, 250
```

The program in Figure 2.2 will draw four rectangles on the screen as shown in Figure 2.3.

```
LineWidth 3
Rectangle 100,100,350,200
Rectangle 400,100,650,200
Rectangle 400,350,650,450
Rectangle 100,350,350,450
End
```

Figure 2.2: This program draws four rectangles.

Study the code of Figure 2.2 carefully and make sure you see how the rectangles are formed. Notice that the width of every rectangle is 250 and the height of every rectangle is 100. Each rectangle is drawn at a different position.

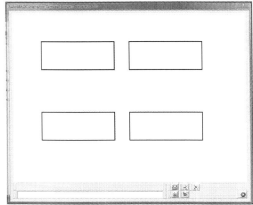

Figure 2.3: These rectangles are created by Figure 2.2.

2.4 Using Variables

For many applications, it would be better if we could specify the size and position of a rectangle (we will see why later) using the variables **x**, **y**, **width**, and **height**. If the values of these variables have already been set, we can draw the rectangle using the following line of code. Notice how the values for the lower-right coordinates are calculated by adding the width and height to the coordinates (x,y) of the upper-left corner.

```
Rectangle x, y, x+width, y+height
```

Notice how the use of variables and *expressions* (calculation formulas) as part of the arguments makes it easier to specify how rectangles are positioned and drawn. If we wanted to draw the four rectangles shown in Figure 2.3 using our new methodology we could use the program in Figure 2.4.

Study the program carefully. Notice how variables are used to control how and where the rectangles are drawn. Let's look at a situation that takes advantage of using variables.

```
LineWidth 3
width = 250
height = 100
x = 100
y = 100
Rectangle x,y,x+width,y+height
x = 400
Rectangle x,y,x+width,y+height
y = 350
Rectangle x,y,x+width,y+height
x = 100
Rectangle x,y,x+width,y+height
End
```

Figure 2.4: This program also draws four Rectangles.

Let's assume you had written the program in Figure 2.4 and then decided that you wanted the rectangles to be squares. We could make this happen for *all* the rectangles by changing only the second line to set the width to 100. Make that change and run the program again. Each of the rectangles should now be a square.

Now let's assume you want to do the same thing with the program in Figure 2.2. Enter this program and make sure it is working properly. Then, change it so that it draws four squares instead of four rectangles. Don't take this assignment lightly. Please take the time to do it. You will be very surprised at how much effort it takes to make the changes when compared to the single change needed for Figure 2.4. As we proceed thorough the book, you will see more and more examples of how variables make programming easier. In fact, let's look at one more example right now.

2.5 User Input
We want to use the program shown in Figure 2.4, but instead of having a prefixed height and width we want the user of the program to be able to specify the height and width of the rectangles. The program in Figure 2.5 shows

how this can be accomplished. Most of the program is exactly the same as in Figure 2.2.

Let's look at some of the new items in the program. The first two Print statements are different. Instead of printing the value of a variable, they are given an argument that is enclosed in quotes. When this is done, the Print command prints the information between the quotes as is.

The next two lines introduce the Input command. When Input is executed, the user is prompted to enter a value inside the input box at the bottom of the terminal screen. The value entered will be stored in the variable specified. In order to tell the user what to do, the text included between the quotes (in the Input statements) is displayed just above the input box. Enter the program shown in Figure 2.5 and run it to see how the Input command works.

When you run the program, you will see the items displayed by the first two Print statements. You will also see the phrase "Enter Width" displayed near the bottom of the screen above the input box. Type a value (e.g. 100) in the box and press the **ENTER** key.

```
Print "This program will draw four rectangles."
Print "It will allow you to specify the width and
height."
Input "Enter Width", width
Input "Enter Height", height
x = 100
y = 100
Rectangle x,y,x+width,y+height
x = 400
Rectangle x,y,x+width,y+height
y = 350
Rectangle x,y,x+width,y+height
x = 100
Rectangle x,y,x+width,y+height
End
```

Figure 2.5: This program lets the user specify the height and width of the rectangles to be drawn.

You will immediately see a new prompt asking you to enter the height. Again enter the number 100. You will then see four rectangles (now squares because the height and width are both 100). Try running the program a few times and enter different values to verify you are actually controlling how the rectangles are being drawn.

2.6 Circles and Ellipses

RobotBASIC has a `Circle` command that is very much like the `Rectangle` command. The arguments for `Circle` define a rectangle just as they did with the `Rectangle` command. Instead of drawing the rectangle though, `Circle` draws a circle (or ellipse) inside the boundaries define by the rectangle. Change any of the `Rectangle` statements in the programs used in this chapter to `Circle` and see what happens when you run them again.

2.7 Using the Robot

Now that we have the ability to draw lines, rectangles, and circles on the screen, we can create objects that our simulated robot has to avoid. Look at the code shown in Figure 2.6 which creates the screen shown in Figure 2.7.

If you understand the concepts we have covered so far, it should be easy to see how the three objects were drawn on the screen. Notice that the robot has been initialized near the center of the screen. Notice also that a *comment* line has been added to show you where you should add your code.

A comment is any line that begins with two slashes (//). Comments (everything on the line past the //) are ignored when the program is executed. They can serve as notes or reminders of why you did certain things or to state the purpose of sections of your code. We will discuss this concept in more detail later in the book.

```
LineWidth 3
Rectangle 200,400,500,550
Circle 200,200,400,300
Line 400,100,700,500
rLocate 350,350
// Enter your code here

End
```

Figure 2.6: This code creates an environment for the robot.

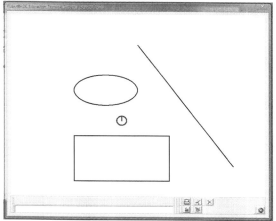

Figure 2.7: You must write code to move the robot to the upper-right corner of the screen.

Your assignment is to use a series of `rTurn` and `rForward` statements to move the robot through the environment with the objective of reaching the upper-right corner of the screen.

Your robot can take any path you wish and turn and forward in any way you want, using as many commands as necessary to complete the task. It is recommend that you enter only one or two new commands though, before running the program to test your code. The reason is that when the robot bumps into any of the objects on the screen (or even one of the exterior walls) it will cause an error. If you get errors, examine your program and make the necessary corrections. The assignment is considered completed when the robot reaches the upper-right corner of the screen without causing an error (which means that it had successfully avoided the objects).

2.8 Summary
In this chapter you have learned:
- ❏ About variables and how they can be used.
- ❏ How to draw rectangles and circles on the terminal screen.
- ❏ How the Input command can allow the user to alter what the program does.
- ❏ How to move the robot through a cluttered environment.

2.9 Exercises
Before moving on to the next chapter, test your knowledge and skill by trying the following exercises. Give each problem your best effort before reviewing the answers given in Appendix A.

1. Enter the program in Figure 2.2 and verify that it runs properly. Add commands to make each of the rectangles a different color.

2. Enter the program in Figure 2.4 and verify that it runs properly. Add commands to make each of the rectangles a different line width.

3. Modify the programs in both Figures 2.2 and 2.4 so that they draw 100 by 100 pixel squares instead of rectangles.

4. Enter the program in Figure 2.5 and verify that it runs properly. Add commands to allow the user to

also specify (with the INPUT command) the x,y position of the *last* rectangle drawn.

5. Enter the program in 2.6 and add your code to move the robot to the upper-right corner of the screen without causing an error.

Chapter 3

Loops

Every program we have written so far has executed the program statements in a sequential order - that is one line after another from beginning to end. The real power of programming though, lies in the ability to control how the execution flows through the program. In some cases we may need to repeatedly execute some lines of code or execute some lines only if certain conditions are satisfied. In this chapter we will see how *loop-structures* can be used to achieve this to help make more powerful and efficient programs.

3.1 Efficiency

Let's start our discussion by examining why loop-structures make a program more efficient. Suppose you owned a tree planting service and hired people to dig the holes to plant the trees. Also assume that you need to give your hole-diggers some instructions. Perhaps they would look something like this:

> Remove one shovel full of dirt.
> Remove one shovel full of dirt.
> Remove one shovel full of dirt.
> ......

Get the idea? The number of shovels of dirt that need to be removed depends, of course, on how big the shovel is, how

---

full they make it, and how big a hole you need. And, who wants to take the time to write the same command dozens or even hundreds of times. Just as this does not make sense in our example of instructions for a hole-digger, it does not make sense for programming either.

3.2 The WHILE–WEND-Structure

What we need is a way of telling the hole-digger (or the computer) how to dig the hole without having to say the same thing so many times. Better instructions for the hole-digger might look something like this:

```
while the hole is less than 2 feet deep
    remove one shovel of dirt
wend
```

The idea is that the indented action must be executed over and over as long as the hole has not reached a depth of two feet. The **wend** (while-end) at the end serves as a marker indicating the end of the **while** loop.

3.3 The REPEAT–UNTIL-Structure

Another way to write the above instructions might look like this:

```
repeat the following
    remove one shovel of dirt
until the hole is 2 feet deep
```

The above example essentially accomplishes the same task as before, but it uses a different approach. In this case the digging continues *until* the hole is deep enough – in the first case the digging continued as long as the whole was *not* deep enough. These may seem the same, but there are some differences.

In the second situation the digger will *always* remove at least one shovel full, even if the hole is already deep enough before he starts. This is true because the decision about whether to continue or not comes at the end of the loop.

In the first example, the decision comes at the beginning, which means if the hole is already deep enough, no dirt will be removed. In most cases, either method will work, but let's examine some situations that make it better, and sometimes even necessary, to use one particular structure rather than the other.

Suppose we were writing instructions on how to pick a ripe apple from a tree. Here are two ways, based on the previous examples.

```
while the apple is not ripe        repeat
    look at a new apple                look at a new apple
wend                               until the apple is ripe
pick the apple                     pick the apple
```

The principle behind both of the examples above is that the loop will continue looking at apples until a ripe apple is found. At that point the looping will stop and execution of the commands continues with the next line, which picks the apple currently being looked at.

In the example on the left, the initial decision makes no sense. How can you decide if an apple is ripe if you have not looked at one yet? This problem is solved in the example on the right because the instructions tell you to look at an apple before you are asked if it is ripe.

Let's look at another example. Suppose you want to eat some grapes. Look at these two methods for accomplishing that task.

```
while you are hungry               repeat
    eat a grape                        eat a gape
wend                               until you are not hungry
```

In this case, the while-structure makes more sense. In the repeat option, you *always* eat a grape even if you are not hungry.

These are simplified examples, but they should illustrate the principles. Creating a loop to cause an action to take place repeatedly (based on some condition) is a very efficient way of handling many tasks. Furthermore, in some cases, we have seen that you must be careful how to construct the loop to ensure that the logic makes sense.

3.4 A Counting-Structure

There is even a third way we could construct a loop. We might give instructions that tell the worker to count the actions and perform them a specific number of times (e.g. the hole-digger should remove exactly 32 shovels of dirt).

3.5 Loops in RobotBASIC

RobotBASIC has ways of creating all three of the above types of loops. You can often use any of them to handle a given situation. As we have seen though, some situations are best handled by a particular type of loop. We will look at some examples here, but future chapters will address looping in more detail.

Remember from last chapter, we saw how to draw a rectangle at a specified spot on the screen. The program in Figure 3.1 will draw 20 rectangles on the screen. We will modify this program several times to demonstrate a variety of looping situations.

```
LineWidth 3
size = 50
for a = 1 to 20
    x = Random(700)
    y = Random(500)
    Rectangle x,y,x+2*size,y+size
    Delay 100
next
End
```

Figure 3.1: This program draws 20 rectangles.

If you have trouble understanding any of the discussions, you should type in the examples and make changes to see what happens when you run the program. This type of interaction will help you learn the material more easily and gain a deeper understanding.

3.6 The FOR-NEXT loop

The program in Figure 3.1 has several new items, so read this section carefully. First, notice the loop itself. It starts with the For statement and ends with the Next statement. This loop provides the counting action mentioned earlier. The lines inside the loop are indented to help you see that they are the portion of the program being repeated. The indenting is not required, but as our programs get more complicated, you will find that proper indenting helps to see how the code is organized and structured.

Before the loop itself, there are two lines. The first sets the line width to 3 and the second gives a value to the variable **size**, which will be used to control the size of the rectangles being drawn (more about this later).

3.7 The Random Function

The first two lines inside the loop introduce the Random function which works like this. We pass a number (the argument in the parenthesis) to Random. Random then acts like a variable with a value equal to some (random) number between (and including) 0 and the number passed (but not including it). In our example, this means that the variable **x** will have a value between (and including) 0 and 699 and the variable **y** will have a value between (and including) 0 and 499.

Since **x** and **y** will have different values every time the loop is executed, the next line in the loop will draw a rectangle (whose width is 2 times **size** and height is equal to **size**) at a different (random) positions.

3.8 The `Delay` Command

The final statement inside the loop is the `Delay` command, which delays the number of milliseconds specified by the argument (100 in this case). This command was added inside the loop to slow the program down so that you could watch the rectangles being drawn. One millisecond is one thousands of a second, so 3000 milliseconds is 3 seconds.

3.9 The `For`-Loop Syntax

Let's now look at the `for`-loop itself. The statement looks like this.

```
For a = 1 to 20
```

This tells the computer to use the variable **a** as a counter. It starts the count at 1 and each time it executes the `Next` statement the value of the variable **a** is incremented by one, then loop starts over at the line right after the `For` statement.

If you would like to see that the variable **a** is actually changing in value, add the following line immediately after the `For` statement.

```
Print a
```

If you add this line, and run the program, you will see a screen similar to the one shown in Figure 3.2. It won't be exactly the same, because the rectangles will be in random positions. The exercises at the end of this chapter will explore other modifications to the program in Figure 3.1.

3.10 Using the Mouse

The `for`-loop is an ideal structure if we know how many times we want a block of code to be executed. In order to demonstrate examples of the `while-wend` and `repeat-until` loops, we will use the `ReadMouse` command. It requires three variables as arguments. An example is shown below.

```
ReadMouse x,y,z
```

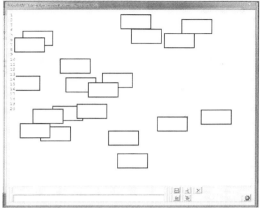

Figure 3.2: Modifying the program in Figure
3.1 makes it display this screen.

When the above `ReadMouse` line is executed, the variables
x and **y** (you can use any variables) will be set to the
current coordinates of the mouse cursor. The variable **z**
will be set to 0 if no buttons on the mouse are pressed, 1 if
the left mouse-button is pressed, and 2 if the right mouse-
button is pressed.

3.11 The `Repeat-Until` Loop

The program in Figure 3.3 will keep drawing rectangles
until the left mouse-button is pressed.

```
LineWidth 3
size = 50
repeat
   x = Random(700)
   y = Random(500)
   Rectangle x,y,x+2*size,y+size
   Delay 100
   ReadMouse a,b,c
until c = 1
End
```

Figure 3.3: This program uses the mouse button
to control how many rectangles are drawn.

Notice that the ReadMouse command is executed at the end of the loop. It uses the variable **c** to obtain the status of the mouse-buttons. The until statement causes the loop to repeat until the left mouse-button is pressed (until **c=1**). If you run this program, rectangles will be drawn continuously until you press the left mouse-button.

Let's see how we could accomplish this same task using the while-loop.

3.12 The While-Wend Loop

The program in Figure 3.4 shows how to draw rectangles until the left mouse-button is pressed (just like before), but this time using a while-wend loop.

Refer to Figure 3.4. The first thing to notice is that the decision in the while is opposite of the decision used in the until statement of Figure 3.3. In this case, the loop *continues while* the button is *NOT* pressed. In Figure 3.3 the loop *quits* if the button *WAS* pressed.

```
LineWidth 3
size = 50
ReadMouse a,b,c
while c = 0
    x = Random(700)
    y = Random(500)
    Rectangle x,y,x+2*size,y+size
    Delay 100
    ReadMouse a,b,c
wend
End
```

Figure 3.4: This program works like Figure 3.3 but it uses a while-wend loop.

It is also important to see that two ReadMouse commands were required in this program. Without the first ReadMouse, the decision in the while makes no sense because the variable **c** does not have a value when the loop first starts. If you remove the first ReadMouse the program will cause an error when the while is first executed because the variable **c** does not yet exist at that point in the program.

This is a good example of when one type of loop is better suited than another. Both the while-wend and the repeat-until loops work here, but the repeat-until is obviously a better choice.

This is a good time to point out that there is no *right-way* to program. There are many ways to accomplish the same task. Often one way might have advantages over another, but if a program performs properly it certainly can't be considered *wrong*. As we proceed through the text you will see ways of making your programs smaller or faster, but as a novice programmer don't worry if you don't immediately see the most efficient choices. That skill will develop as you write more and more programs.

3.13 Error Messages

In each of these loop structures, there is a beginning and an end to the loop (for-next, repeat-until, while-wend). If you forget to end a loop, RobotBASIC may not issue any type of error. To demonstrate this, remove the wend statement from Figure 3.4.

Even though the program is expecting a wend statement, it will execute the End statement when it comes to it and the program will terminate, but no error has been issued. This is just one example of how programming errors can be difficult to find. This subject will be addressed in more detail in later chapters.

3.14 Summary

In this chapter you have learned:
- ❑ That loops can make programming more efficient.
- ❑ The three types of loops available in RobotBASIC.

❑ How to use loop-structures to implement a task.

❑ About `Random`, `Delay` and `ReadMouse`.

3.15 Exercises

Before moving on to the next chapter, test your knowledge and skill by trying the following exercises. Give each problem your best effort before reviewing the answers given in Appendix A.

1. Modify the program in Figure 3.1 so that it draws only 10 rectangles. Change it again to get 30 rectangles.

2. Modify the program in Figure 3.1 so that the rectangles are taller than they are wide.

> **Hint:** You have to modify how the width and height are established.

3. Modify the program in Figure 3.1 so that the colors of the rectangles are chosen at random.

> **Hint:** Even though we have referred to colors by name, RobotBASIC automatically substitutes a number from 0 to 15 for the colors (see the CONSTANTS help page). Place the following command at an appropriate place inside the loop.
> ```
> SetColor Random(15)
> ```

4. Modify the program in Figure 3.1 so the size of the rectangles is a random number between 50 and 200.

> **Hint:** Place the following command at an appropriate place inside the loop.
> ```
> size = Random(150)+50
> ```
> Can you explain how this new line accomplishes its goal?

Chapter 4

Making Decisions

In the last chapter we saw how portions of a program can be repeated using loop structures. In this chapter we will see how a program can make decisions about which sections of code to execute.

The principal decision-making command in RobotBASIC is the `if` statement which has many formats. We will cover three formats in this chapter.

4.1 The `if-then` Structure

The simplest form of the `if` statement is a one-line structure that looks like this:

> if **expression** then **statement**

When the above line is executed, the **expression** is tested to see if it is true and if it is, then the **statement** is executed. If the **expression** is not true, the **statement** will not be executed.

4.2 The `if-endif` Structure

The `if-then` structure has its limitation. The most obvious of these is that only one statement can be executed if the

---

expression is true. The `if-endif` structure solves this problem. Its general format looks like this:

```
if expression
    // if the expression is true
    // do all the statements
    // between the if
    // and the endif
endif
// if the expression is false
// execution continues here
```

If the **expression** is true, then all of the statements that lie between the `if` and the `endif` are executed. If the **expression** is false, then none of the statements are executed and the program continues execution at the line after the `endif`.

4.3 The `if-else-endif` Structure

This structure is the most versatile of the three discussed here. It takes the form below:

```
if expression
    // if the expression is true
    // do all these statements
else
    // if the expression is false
    // do all these statements
endif
```

This structure allows the program to decide which of two blocks of statements are executed, based on whether the expression is true or false.

4.4 Typical Expressions

Now that you know the three formats that `if` statements can take, let's look at some examples of the **expression**. Figure 4.1 shows some simple expressions and the conditions that make them true.

This Expression	is True if
x = 3	x has a value of 3
x < > 4	x is not equal to 4
x > 8	x is greater than 8
a < x	a is less than x
a=2 and b>-3	a equals 2 and b is greater than -3
a<x or b<20	a is less than x or b is less than 20
x	x is anything other than zero

Figure 4.1: Sample expressions and the conditions that make them true.

4.5 A Simple Example

Let's look at an example to demonstrate how a program can make decisions about the things it is doing. We want a program to choose 20 random positions on the screen and draw either a circle or a square at the chosen position based on the following condition. If the position chosen is on the top-half of the screen, a circle should be drawn. If the position is on the bottom-half, then a square should be drawn. The program in Figure 4.2 accomplishes this task.

The program in Figure 4.2 is very similar to the examples in Chapter 3, so it should be easy to follow. The for-loop executes its contents 20 times. Each time through the loop, random coordinates are chosen. If the **y** portion of the coordinates is less than 300 then the position is on the top half of the screen and a circle is drawn, otherwise, a square is drawn.

Suppose we want the circles to be on the bottom half of the screen and the squares on the top. One way to achieve this is to swap the two lines (Circle and Rectangle), but an easier way is to change the expression in the if statement to y > 300. Make this change and verify that the program performs as expected.

Can you predict how the program will draw if the `if` expression was changed to `x < 400`?

```
LineWidth 3
size = 50
for c = 1 to 20
    x = random(700)
    y = random(500)
    if y<300
        Circle x,y,x+2*size,y+size
    else
        Rectangle x,y,x+size,y+size
    endif
    Delay 100
next
end
```

Figure 4.2: This program draws circles and squares.

4.6 Nested `if` Statements

It is possible to put one `if` statement inside another. This is called *nesting*. In fact, putting the `if`-structures inside the loop-structures is also a form of nesting.

The program of Figure 4.2 used an `if-else-endif` structure to determine if the chosen position was on the top or bottom of the screen. We could put another `if-else-endif` in both of the sections of the original `if` structure. These new `if` statements could decide if the position is on the left or right side of the screen, and draw the shapes in different colors depending on the side chosen. Figure 4.3 shows how this can be done.

Notice how the new `if` statements are further indented. Again, this is not required, but is highly recommended because it helps the programmer visualize the various blocks of code and more easily see the conditions affecting when each is performed.

```
LineWidth 3
size = 50
for c = 1 to 20
    x = random(700)
    y = random(500)
    if y<300
        if x<400
            SetColor Blue
        else
            SetColor Red
        endif
        Circle x,y,x+2*size,y+size
    else
        if x<400
            SetColor Green
        else
            SetColor Black
        endif
        Rectangle x,y,x+size,y+size
    endif
    Delay 100
next
end
```

Figure 4.3: This program uses nested control structures.

Notice also how the new `if` statements cause the colors to be changed and let the original `Circle` and `Rectangle` commands do the actual work of drawing the shapes.

Study the program in Figure 4.3 carefully. Act as if you are the computer and work your way through the program one line at a time. Notice how you navigate through the program after you have chosen a random value for the variables **x** and **y**.

4.7 Expressions in Loops
We have seen how expressions can be used to control how a program executes various statements or blocks of statements. It is important to recognize that all the expressions used in

if statements can also be used as arguments for while and until statements.

In the chapters that follow we will use loops and if decisions to give our programs the ability to deal with complex applications on their own. You may be surprised at how intelligent a system can become if we program it properly.

4.8 Summary

In this chapter you have learned:

- ❑ That loops and if structures can alter the execution order of statements in a program.
- ❑ About three different if structures.
- ❑ About the expressions used in decision statements.
- ❑ How control structures can be nested inside each other.

4.9 Exercises

Before moving on to the next chapter, test your knowledge and skill by trying the following exercises. Give each problem your best effort before reviewing the answers given in Appendix A.

1. Enter and test the programs discussed in this chapter.

2. Modify the program of Figure 4.2 so that it draws green circles on the left side of the screen and red squares on the right side.

3. Modify the program of Figure 4.2 so that each of the shapes being drawn is of a random size.

4. Modify the program of Figure 4.3 so that the circles are in the upper-right and lower-left corners and the rectangles are in the upper-left and lower-right corners.

Chapter 5

Using the Mouse

Previous chapters have shown you a little about loops and decision structures. In this chapter we will utilize all the knowledge you have gained so far to create some simple applications that are more interesting than the examples discussed up until now.

5.1 Using Mouse Buttons to Control Shapes

Let's start with a simple but interesting example. Our goal is to write a program that allows you to move the mouse cursor around the screen. At any time you can click the left or right mouse button to draw a shape at the current mouse position.

If you press the left button, a square will be drawn. The right button will draw a circle. The program in Figure 5.1 will perform these actions.

There are several details to notice about the program in Figure 5.1. First, the `while`-loop in the program is endless. The decision-expression for the `while` is just **True** (an internal constant). Since the argument is *always* true the statements inside the `while` will execute continuously until you close the program manually (clicking the ⊠ in the upper-right corner).

```
LineWidth 3
size = 50
while True
    ReadMouse x,y,b
    if b=1 then Rectangle x,y,x+size,y+size
    if b=2 then Circle x,y,x+size,y+size
wend
end
```

Figure 5.1: This program uses the mouse buttons to draw different shapes.

The two `if-then` statements inside the loop check to see if the left or right mouse button is pressed and if either is, then the appropriate shape is drawn.

When the shapes are drawn they are positioned according to the variables **x** and **y,** which are assigned by the `ReadMouse` command according to the mouse position.

5.2 Drawing with the Mouse

When you run the program in Figure 5.1 move the mouse cursor to a place where you want to draw a shape. Click the left mouse button if you want to draw a rectangle or the right mouse button if you want to draw a circle. You will see the selected shape draw on the screen using the size specified in the program.

If you hold down one of the mouse keys while moving the mouse, the program will continually draw the selected shape. This means the mouse will leave a trail of shapes as it moves as shown in Figure 5.2.

5.3 A Simple Animation

After you try drawing trails with the program in Figure 5.1 add a `ClearScr` command immediately following the last `if` statement. This new command clears the screen, which means the "old" version of the shape is constantly erased. Since you only see the "new" version, the selected shape will follow the mouse cursor around the screen as you move the mouse (assuming a button is pressed).

This illusion of movement (it is an illusion because *one* shape is not moving – you see a *new* shape in a different spot) will be the basis for some interesting programs in later chapters.

Figure 5.2: Moving the mouse while holding down a button creates interesting trails.

5.4 Two Sizes of Shapes

At this point you know enough about programming for us to start doing some interesting applications. The program in Figure 5.3 gives us the capability to use the mouse to change the size of the shapes being drawn while the program is running.

It uses two new statements. Let's start by examining them. The first of these statements is a function called `Within()` that must be given three arguments as shown in the example below.

```
Within (x, y, 100)
```

Since `Within()` is a function, it takes on a value just like a variable. The value will either be **True** or **False**. For the example above, `Within()` will be **True** if the value of the variable **x** is between the value for the variable **y** and 100. If it is outside this range, `Within()` will be **False**.

Another new statement in this program is the command `xyString`. It is very much like `Print`, except that we can specify an **x,y** coordinate indicating where on the screen the printing should take place.

Now we are ready to examine the program in Figure 5.3, which is an enhanced version of the one shown in Figure 5.1. Make sure you fully understand Figure 5.1 before you continue.

The additions to the program demonstrate how a mouse can be used to select options. Notice that comments have been provided throughout the program to help you understand the code.

The lines near the top of the program draw two rectangles, one at the top-left and one at the top-right corners of the screen. The `xyString` command is used to print the words **small** and **large** inside these rectangles.

The variable **size** is set to 50 (the default value for a large shape) and the word **large** is printed at the top-center of the screen to indicate to the user the current size.

Let's move inside the `while`-loop to see how the real work is done. The first `if` statement checks to see if the mouse cursor is at the top of the screen (the value of **y** is between 0 and 50, the height of our rectangular buttons). If it is, further decisions have to be made (see the next paragraph) but if the cursor is not at the top of the screen, a square or circle is drawn just like Figure 5.1.

If the cursor is at the top of the page, two `if` statements are used to determine if the **x**-value of the mouse position lies within the horizontal position of either of the two rectangular buttons drawn earlier. When these `if` statements determine that a valid request has been made, the variable **size** is set to either 15 or 50 (which will make future shapes draw at this new size). Notice also that the word **large** or **small** is printed at the top of the screen to indicate to the user that the selected size has been set.

```
LineWidth 3
// Draw two rectangles
// label them small and large
SetColor Red
Rectangle 0,0,70,50
xyString 15,20,"small"
Rectangle 730,0,799,50
xyString 740,20,"large"
// setup default size
size = 50
xyString 350,20,"LARGE"
while True
    ReadMouse x,y,b
    // see if mouse is at top of screen
    // with a button pressed
    if Within(y,0,50) and (b=1 or b=2)
        if Within(x,0,70)
            // top and left
            size = 15
            xyString 350,20,"SMALL"
        endif
        if Within(x,730,799)
            // top and right
            size = 50
            xyString 350,20,"LARGE"
        endif
    else
        // not at top so check for drawing
        if b=1 then Rectangle x,y,x+size,y+size
        if b=2 then Circle x,y,x+size,y+size
    endif
wend
end
```

Figure 5.3: This program demonstrates how to use the `ReadMouse` command.

5.5 Using the Enhanced Program

If you enter and run the program in Figure 5.3 you can draw individual shapes by pressing either the left or right mouse buttons, or leave a trail by holding down a button while moving the mouse. At any time, you can click one of the two rectangular buttons in the top-corners of the screen to select a new size to use. Figure 5.4 shows a sample screen with various actions taken.

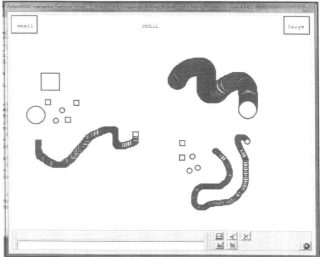

Figure 5.4: The program in Figure 5.3 was used to create this screen.

5.6 Summary

In this chapter you have learned:

- How to utilize the coordinates and button information from `ReadMouse`.
- How to create "buttons" that can be "pressed" with the mouse.
- How to create an animated movement on the screen.
- How to draw with the mouse.
- Two new commands, `Within` and `xyString`.

5.7 Exercises

Before moving on to the next chapter, test your knowledge and skill by trying the following exercises. Give each problem your best effort before reviewing the answers given in Appendix A.

1. If you run the program of Figure 5.3, you will notice it draws in Red. Can you explain why? Fix the program so that it draws in Black, but everything drawn at the top of the screen remains in Red.

2. Modify the program of Figure 5.3 so that it has a third button (anywhere you want) that allows you to choose a MEDIUM sized shape.

3. Modify the program of Figure 5.3 so the program draws a large + sign instead of a square.

> ✒ **Hint:** Draw two lines to make the + sign. The arguments for the lines should be based on **x**, **y**, and **size** as shown below. Make sure you analyze these lines and understand how they work.
> ```
> Line x,y,x,y+size
> s = size/2
> Line x-s,y+s,x+s,y+s
> ```

Chapter 6

A Smarter Robot

Chapters 1 and 2 introduced the simulated robot. In this chapter we will give the robot some intelligence. The robot is actually much more advanced than we can cover in this introductory text. It has many sensors (including a compass, a GPS, infrared object detection, ultrasonic distance measurement and many others) that can be analyzed using if statements. In this book, we will only utilize the robot's bumpers.

6.1 Bumper Switches

Imagine if we had a real robot and wanted it to be able to determine when it bumped into an object. We might place switches around the perimeter of the robot and build an electronic circuit that could allow the controlling computer to determine if those switches have been pressed (due to bumping into an object).

The simulated robot has four switches mounted around its perimeter. There is one in front, one in the back and one on each side. RobotBASIC has a function called rBumper() that checks the status of these switches and gives us a number that indicates which switch has contacted an object according to the following table.

Number	Switch Pressed
1	Rear
2	Right side
4	Front
8	Left side

If two switches are pressed, the number given by rBumper() will be the sum of the numbers for each switch. An example should help clarify these ideas. If we wanted our program to check to see if the front bumper has contacted some object, we could use the following code.

```
if rBumper() = 4
    // do the appropriate
    // actions here
endif
```

Of course, we could test rBumper() with any format of the if statement or with the while or until statements.

6.2 Designing a Program

Let's design a program that gives our robot a little more intelligence. The first step is to decide exactly what we want the robot to do.

We want the robot to move forward until it hits an object. At that point, we want the robot to turn away from that object. If we put both of these actions inside an endless loop, the robot should wander aimlessly around its environment. A program to perform these actions is shown in Figure 6.1.

6.3 Explaining the Program

After the robot is located near the center of the screen, an endless while-loop keeps the robot moving. The second while-loop causes the robot to inch its way forward. If none of the bumpers are pressed (rBumper()=0) then the robot moves forward one pixel.

```
// create the robot near the
// center of the screen
rLocate 400,300
while True
    //move forward till bumped
    while rBumper()=0
        rForward 1
    wend
    // back up one pixel
    rforward -1
    // now turn away
    rTurn 180
wend
end
```

Figure 6.1: This robot can avoid a wall.

This action makes sure that the robot never moves more than one pixel before checking the bumper switches again. This is important because the robot will cause an error if it continues to move even a few pixels toward an object or wall *after* the bumper has been pressed. You can see this by simply making the robot move forward five pixels at a time instead of one.

As long as the robot has not bumped an object, execution of the program will stay inside the second while-loop. When an object is encountered, the loop will terminate and execution will continue to the statements following the wend. The first thing we make the robot do is back up one pixel (go forward a negative number). This makes sure it is away from the wall so that none of the sensor switches are being pressed. Next, rTurn causes the robot to turn 180°, making the robot turn around and face in exactly the opposite direction that it was moving.

If you enter and run the program, the robot will continually move back and forth between the top and bottom walls. Not very exciting! Add the following statement immediately before the first while statement.

```
rTurn 20
```

The robot now moves at an angle, but it still repeats the same actions over and over. Let's see why.

6.4 Improving the Program

Each time a bumper hits an object, the robot turns around completely. The important thing to realize here is that this happens no matter which bumper is hit. Our robot would seem a lot more intelligent if it checked to see which bumper was hit and properly turned away from the object causing the problem. For example, if the left bumper is hit, the robot should turn right. If the right bumper is hit, the robot should turn left. Figure 6.2 shows a program that *tries* to do this.

Let's see how the program is supposed to work. Instead of just turning 180°, the robot now uses three if statements to determine which way it should turn. If the front bumper is pressed, then it turns 180° just as it did before.

Unfortunately, this program does not work. Actually it has several problems. Finding out why programs don't work is a very important aspect of programming called *debugging*. So important in fact, that the rest of this chapter will be devoted to finding out why the program is not doing what we expect it to do, and then fixing the problem. By the time we fix all the problems, the robot, and you, should be a lot smarter.

6.5 Finding the Problem

If you run the program shown in Figure 6.2 the robot will move forward until it hits the wall and then just keep going backwards and forwards one pixel. The reason for the failure is not obvious, especially to someone new to programming. Analyze the program and see if you can find the problem. Don't be surprised if you can't. The examples that follow will help you learn how to logically find problems in a program.

```
// create the robot near the
// center of the screen
rLocate 400,300
rTurn 20
while True
    // move forward till bumped
    while rBumper()=0
       rForward 1
    wend
    // back up one pixel
    rForward -1
    //now turn away
    if rBumper() = 2 then rTurn -90
    if rBumper() = 8 then rTurn 90
    if rBumper() = 4 then rTurn 180
wend
end
```

Figure 6.2: This program does not operate properly.

Run the program again and watch the robot carefully. Notice it *never* turns away from the wall. It seems that the if statements are never becoming true. In order to try to find out why, put the following statement right after the comment (// now turn away).

                    Print rBumper()

Run the program again. The robot stalls just like before, but now we see zero being printed over and over on the left side of the screen. This gives us a clue that the rBumper() function is saying that no switches are being bumped. Now we have something concrete to think about.

If you study the program long enough, you will find the answer. Remember, when the robot hit the wall, we made it move away from it (rForward -1). This means that no bumpers are currently being pressed. You might think that we could just not move the robot away from the wall, but that won't work either. If we just turn without backing up one of the other switches might be touching the wall and the robot won't move forward (because the while that makes it move forward will be false and the rForward command will not be executed).

How can we solve this problem? One solution is to make the robot *remember* which bumpers were pressed just prior to backing away. We can do this by storing the rBumper() value inside a variable. The program in Figure 6.3 shows how to do this.

Examine the program and note how the variable **bump** is made equal to the value of the rBumper() function. Notice also that this is done *before* the robot moves away from the wall.

Since the variable **bump** remembers what the bumper conditions were before the robot moved away from the wall, we can change the three if statements to check **bump** instead of rBumper().

The program in Figure 6.3 is an improvement, but it is far from what we want. After the robot hits the top wall, it turns a full 180° and heads downward. When it hits the bottom wall it again turns completely around and heads upward. This process continues in an endless loop.

```
// create the robot near the
// center of the screen
rLocate 400,300
rTurn 20
while True
    // move forward till bumped
    while rBumper()=0
      rForward 1
    wend
    bump = rBumper()
    // back up one pixel
    rForward -1
    // now turn away
    if bump = 2  then rTurn -130
    if bump = 8  then rTurn 130
    if bump = 4 then rTurn 180
wend
end
```

Figure 6.3: This program is better, but it still does not work properly.

The reason the robot never turns 90° or -90°, of course, is that the robot has to hit the wall at a steep angle in order to make contact with one of the side bumpers, and this never happens. If the robot turns completely around (180°) whenever it hits the front bumper this repeating action will always occur. What we need is a way to make the robot turn around when it hits the front bumper, but not always 180°.

6.6 Adding Randomness

We could just make the robot turn 160° or any value other than 180°, but we know from an earlier chapter how to generate a random number, so let's try that. If you replace the last if statement with the following line, the program responds a little better.

```
if bump = 4 then rTurn 140+random(80)
```

The function random(80) will generate a number between 0 and 80. When we add that to 140, the robot will always turn somewhere between 140° and 220°. This is a complete turn around ± 40° degrees.

The modified program seems to work well for a short while. The robot does in fact turn away a random amount from a front collision. If you watch the robot carefully, you will see that when it hits one of the side bumpers it turns directly left or right, just as we planned. Unfortunately though, if you wait long enough, the robot eventually gets stuck.

You can try changing the rTurn statement at the beginning of the program so that the robot starts off in some different initial direction, but no matter what angle you try the robot will eventually get stuck somewhere. Can you figure out why?

The reason is not obvious, so let's again add a print statement to give us more information. Think of the error as if it is a crime and you are the detective. The print statement is one way of getting some extra clues to help you solve the crime. Add the following line just before the first `if` statement.

```
print bump
```

Now when the robot gets stuck we can see what number is being reported by the `rBumper()` function. Depending on what your initial turn is (at the beginning of the program) you will get numbers like 12 or 6, maybe even 14 (depending on where the robot gets stuck). As you recall, if more than one bumper is pressed simultaneously then the number reported by `rBumper()` is the sum of the individual bumper numbers.

The number 12 means that both the left and front bumpers are triggered. A 6 implies the front and right bumpers have been hit together. If the robot just happens to wedge in a corner just right, we might even get 14 indicating the front and both sides have all been triggered. When this happens the program fails because our program does not consider these possibilities. One possible way to correct this problem is to replace the three `if` statements with the following lines:

```
if bump =2 or bump =6  then rTurn -130
if bump =8 or bump =12 then rTurn 130
if bump =4 or bump =14 then rTurn 140+random (80)
```

These lines make sure that the robot knows how to respond no matter which bumpers are triggered. The modified program seems to work okay, but what if there were objects in the room with the robot so that there is something to bump into besides the walls. We already know how to do this (refer to Figure 5.1 in Chapter 5).

6.7 Adding Obstacles in the Room

The program in Figure 6.4 combines the object drawing ability discussed in Chapter 5 with the bumper capability covered in this chapter.

The program in Figure 6.4 has only a few additions over the one discussed earlier. At the beginning of the program, two lines were added to set the variable **size** and the width of the lines for the shapes.

Later in the program the mouse conditions are read using ReadMouse and a square or circle is drawn if one of the buttons are pressed. This should be clear to you if you understood Chapter 5. What may be a little confusing is *where* this code was added.

```
// create the robot near the
// center of the screen
size = 50
LineWidth 3
rLocate 400,300
rTurn 20
while True
    // move forward till bumped
    while rBumper()=0
        rForward 1
        // draw an object if mouse is clicked
        ReadMouse x,y,b
        if b=1 then Rectangle x,y,x+size,y+size
        if b=2 then Circle x,y,x+size,y+size
    wend
    bump = rBumper()
    // back up one pixel
    rForward -1
    // now turn away
    if bump = 2 or bump = 6 then rTurn -130
    if bump = 8 or bump = 12 then rTurn 130
    if bump = 4 or bump = 14 then rTurn 140+random(80)
wend
end
```

Figure 6.4: Now the robot can avoid obstacles in the room.

Notice that the original program had two nested while-loops. The interior loop moved the robot forward as long as the robot did not hit an object. This means that the program spends nearly all of its time in this loop, moving the robot forward. If we did not place the ReadMouse code (along with the two if statements that handle the drawing of the shapes) inside this loop we would have to hold the mouse buttons down until the robot hits an object in order to get the new code to execute. Try moving the `ReadMouse` code just below the interior `while`-loop and run the program to see what happens.

There is a very important concept introduced by this program. Two completely different actions are taking place simultaneously (the robot is moving and you are drawing shapes). In fact, the program is only doing one of these things at a time but by placing the code for the two actions properly inside loops, both actions appear concurrent to the user. Later chapters will deal with this idea in more detail.

6.8 Testing the New Program

If you enter the program in Figure 6.4 and run it, you can click the mouse at any time to draw a circle or a square. You can even hold down a button to draw a trail of circles or squares.

If you create an overly cluttered environment for the robot though, problems can occur. The screen-shot in Figure 6.5 shows an example environment that caused a problem.

As you can see from the figure, several shapes and barriers have been drawn and the robot has found its way into a tight spot. Notice also that an error message has been issued indicating that the robot has collided with an object. We could get more clues by using another `print` statement, but if you are starting to understand how our robot works you might already have guessed the problem. The code never checks to see if the back bumper has been hit, so the robot might back into an object, causing a collision.

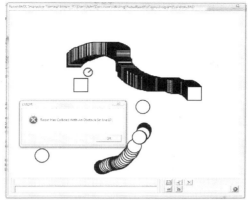

Figure 6.5: The robot fails in a complex environment.

6.9 Handling the Backup Problem

It is actually pretty easy to fix the program so the robot does not back into an object. We just need for the robot to check the back bumper and make sure it is not triggered before it backs up. Just replace the command rForward -1 with the following line:

```
if bump <> 1 then rForward -1
```

This line checks to see if the bumper value is NOT equal to the number 1 (meaning the back bumper is NOT triggered). To be totally safe, we should also check to make sure it is not equal to 9 (the back and left sensors) or 3 (the back and right sensor) or even 11 (the back and both sides). How detailed we must be with our checking really depends on how complex the robot's environment might be.

That is the problem with building real robots that have to deal with the real world. If we don't want our creations to crash when unusual situations are encountered we have to fine-tune our programs. The better we are at anticipating the problems our robot must face, the better we can be at programming our robot to react intelligently.

One of the nice things about having a simulator like RobotBASIC is that you can play with complex ideas and learn a lot about programming a robot without spending a lot of money and time creating a physical model (which might end up destroying itself when your faulty program topples it down a flight of stairs).

The RobotBASIC robot actually is far more powerful than we have shown in this introductory book. As mentioned earlier, it has many other sensors that allow you experiment with very complex situations. If you want to learn more about the simulator read through the RobotBASIC Help files or check out the book *Robot Programmer's Bonanza*, published by McGraw-Hill. You can read more about it at www.RobotBASIC.com.

You should also know that RobotBASIC has many other methods to help you find errors in your program. For example, if your program stops due to an error, you can see the value of every variable by choosing *View Variable Table* from the *RUN* menu. Also, research the Debug command in the Help files to learn more about finding errors.

6.10 Our Robot Can Draw

Before leaving this chapter, let's explore one more feature of our robot. The simulated robot has a "pen" mounted at its center that can be raised and lowered to the floor so that it leaves a mark (trail) as it moves, using the following commands.

```
rPen Up
rPen Down
```

However, there is a problem with having the robot draw a line as it moves. If the robot encounters the line it is drawing it will think it is an object in the room. We can fix this by telling the robot that the color used for the line is invisible, that is, the color should not be seen as an object. We do this with the rInvisible command. We just give it a color to ignore which will also be the color automatically used by the robot's pen. Check the Help files if you want to learn more about these features.

If you add the following two lines immediately after the `rLocate` command in the program of Figure 6.4, the robot will leave a trail and you will be able to see the path it takes while avoiding objects in the room.

```
rInvisible Green
rPen Down
```

6.11 Summary
In this Chapter you have learned:
- ❏ About the simulated robot's bumper switches.
- ❏ How a program's design can be faulty.
- ❏ How programming errors can be analyzed, found and corrected.
- ❏ How multiple tasks can be carried out simultaneously.
- ❏ How the robot can be commanded to leave a trail.

6.12 Exercises
Before moving on to the next chapter, test your knowledge and skill by trying the following exercises. Give each problem your best effort before reviewing the answers given in Appendix A.

1. Modify the final program in this Chapter by experimenting with the amount of randomness in the turns. See if you can make the robot navigate more smoothly through its environment.

2. Test the programs in this chapter and see if you can find environmental situations that cause the robot to fail. If so, try to investigate and solve the problem.

3. If you have enjoyed programming the robot, read about the `rFeel()` function in the Help Files and

modify the programs in this chapter so they use this function instead of `rBumper()`.

4. Read about `rPen` in the Help files and experiment with the robot drawing lines of different colors. Do not forget to assign these colors as invisible using the `rInvisible` command.

Chapter 7

Modular Programming

Any program that you write will be composed of sections that perform one or more functions. In all the programs we have developed so far, the sections were very informal. In this chapter we are going to explore the advantages of using functional modules to better organize the programs we write.

7.1 Subroutines and Labels

The modules we create in RobotBASIC are called *subroutines* and have the format shown below.

```
NameOfModule:
    // place some code here
    // as many lines as you need
Return
```

The name of the module is referred to as a *label*. Labels are case sensitive (like variables) and must be followed by a colon. The code inside the module is usually indented to help identify where it starts and stops. The module must end with a `Return` statement.

7.2 The `Gosub` Command

Your program can execute the code contained in a subroutine module by calling it with the following statement.

```
Gosub NameOfModule
```

The name of the module is *not* followed by the colon when used with a `Gosub` command. When execution in the subroutine reaches the `Return` statement, execution is transferred back to the line following the `Gosub` statement that originally called the subroutine.

7.3 Advantages of Modular Programming

Consider for a moment how a large company is organized. The president of the company decides *what* needs to be done in order to achieve the company's goals. The president does not have to know the details of *how* to accomplish many of the tasks that have to be done because there are vice-presidents that handle the details for him.

Let's look at an example. Suppose the president decides the company needs to add a product to their product line. The president goes to the head of manufacturing and asks what changes need to be made to the company's plants and uses that information to command the head of finance to calculate how much new money the company will need as well as alternatives for how the money can be raised. The head of marketing will be responsible for creating an advertising campaign for the new product. The list could go on and on, but you get the idea.

In fact, even the vice presidents don't need to know exactly how to accomplish the respective goals. They have sub-managers and those sub-managers have workers – the people that ultimately do all the work. Everyone above the workers is responsible, not for work, but for decisions, planning, organization and so forth.

This does not mean that the managers are not important. On the contrary, this organizational structure lets each departmental area focus on their tasks and their needs without worrying about other aspects of the project. It is a divide-and-conquer strategy that turns a large project into many simple ones.

7.4 Organizing a Program

Programs, especially large programs, need to be organized in the manner described above. Subroutines allow you to combine all the code needed to perform a task and give it a name related to that task. The main portion of your program acts like a manager, calling subroutines when needed to get the job done.

Much of the code in a program organized this way will be responsible to for deciding *what* needs to be done and *when* it should be done. Subroutines are called to do the actual work.

The decision portions of a program are composed of control structures like loops and `if` statements. When you write that part of your program you don't have to worry about *how* anything is done because you assume you have subroutines (just like workers) that can handle the tasks you assign them.

Conversely, when you write the subroutines, you don't have to worry about anything other than solving some specific problem or carrying out some specific task, and if the problem or task is too complex, just write the subroutine as if it is a mid-level manager (that can divide the complex problem into smaller tasks) and let it call other subroutines to handle the actual work.

This is a powerful structure that makes programming much easier. Let's look at an example to demonstrate how modular programming can be implemented. Examine the program in Figure 7.1. It is a modularized version of the program we wrote in Chapter 6 (see Figure 6.4).

7.5 Analyzing the Program

Let's look first at the main portion of the program. The program starts with the main-program which is followed by the subroutines. The main-program MUST always come first. Notice how the code has been indented to make it easy to see that it is a special section of the program.

Notice also how easy it is to see an overview of the program's operation by looking *only* at this section.

We see that the program first performs some initialization tasks. We don't know what these tasks are but we know that all programs probably have to do some kind of initialization. The point is, we will worry about the details of this module later as we develop the program. At this point, we are only approaching the problem as a manager.

After the initialization, the main program consists of a loop that repeats three actions over and over. These actions are:

- The robot moves forward until it hits something.
- The robot backs up a little.
- The robot turns away from the object it hit.

This makes it very easy to see how our program works. There are three tasks that have to be addressed. We can turn our attention to each of these tasks, one at a time, and decide how to accomplish each one without having to worry about the others. Let's look at each of these tasks individually. We will examine the easy ones first.

7.6 Backing Up
The **BackUp** module makes the robot back away from the wall or other objects, but, as we saw in Chapter 6, it should not back up if there is an object behind the robot.

7.7 Drawing an Object
At the beginning of the design phase we decided we wanted the user to be able to draw circles and squares on the screen. The **DrawObject** module must read the mouse information and use that to draw the selected object at the current mouse position if a mouse button is pressed.

```
// Main Program (MUST always come first)
   gosub Initialization
   while True
      gosub ForwardTillCollision
      gosub BackUp
      gosub TurnAway
   wend
end

Initialization:
   size = 50
   LineWidth 3
   rLocate 400,300
   rTurn 20
Return

BackUp:
   // backs up only if nothing behind
   if rBumper() <> 1 then rForward -1
Return

ForwardTillCollision:
   // move forward till bumped
   while rBumper()=0
      rForward 1
      gosub DrawObject
   wend
   // sets value of the variable bump for TurnAway
   bump = rBumper()
Return

DrawObject:
   // draw only if a button is pressed
   ReadMouse x,y,b
   if b=1 then Rectangle x,y,x+size,y+size
   if b=2 then Circle x,y,x+size,y+size
Return

TurnAway:
   // assumes bump equals bumper data from collision
   if bump = 2 or bump = 6 then rTurn -130
   if bump = 8 or bump = 12 then rTurn 130
   if bump = 4 or bump = 14 then rTurn 140+random(80)
Return
```

Figure 7.1: Modular programming provides organization.

7.8 Turning Away from the Collision

When the robot strikes an object, we want it to turn away from the object. When designing the program initially, we might not know exactly how we want to do this (how much randomness to use, or which bumpers are important) but we can decide those things when **TurnAway** is actually written.

We do know that **TurnAway** will need information about what bumpers were triggered during the collision so we will assume that this information has been stored in the variable **bump**.

7.9 Moving Forward Until a Collision

The module **ForwardTillCollision** has to perform several tasks. It must move forward until it strikes an object but while it is doing so it needs to draw any object that the user requests. Since this module does not need to be concerned with how objects are drawn, it assumes there is another routine called **DrawObject** that can handle the task. Notice how this delegation makes this module easy to understand and easy to write.

The **DrawObject** module terminates once an object has been encountered. Before termination though, this module stores the bumper data in **bump** (so it can be used later by **TurnAway**). We will discuss **bump** further later.

7.10 Drawing Objects

The module **DrawObject** has to check the mouse to see if the user has pressed a mouse-button indicating they want to draw a shape. If a button has been pressed, the module will draw the desired shape at the current mouse position.

7.11 More Advantages

Hopefully you are starting to see how modular organization helps to create a program that is easy to design and understand. The overall program is slightly longer, but it is much easier to understand and modify.

Suppose, for example, that after the program has been written, you decided you wanted to be able to draw a different shape instead of the circle. Because of the program's organization you know exactly where to go in the program to make the necessary changes (the **DrawObject** module).

Modular organization also helps you find programming errors. When a program is properly structured, it is often easy to isolate a fault to a particular module just based on what happens when the program fails. If, for example, the robot does not stop when it comes to an object we know the problem is most likely in the **ForwardTillCollision** module, because that is the module that has the responsibility for stopping the robot when it encounters an object. This ability to narrow down where the error might be can be a great help, especially for very large programs.

All the programs discussed in later chapters will use modular programming techniques to make them easier to understand. After a little exposure to this idea you will find it hard to imagine programs written in any other way.

7.12 Summary

In this chapter you have learned:

- ❑ What modular programming is and why it is important.
- ❑ How subroutines and `gosub` statements can be used to implement modular programming.
- ❑ How modular programming improves the design process.
- ❑ How modular programming makes it easier to find errors.
- ❑ How to convert the program of Chapter 6 to a modular one.

7.13 Exercises

Before moving on to the next chapter, test your knowledge and skill by trying the following exercises. Give each problem your best effort before reviewing the answers given in Appendix A.

1. Study the program in Figure 7.1 carefully. Make sure you see how each module handles its assigned tasks as well as how the main program calls each module when it is needed.

2. Select a program from a previous chapter and modify its structure so that it uses subroutines.

Chapter 8

Animation

With all the skills and experience gained from the previous seven chapters, you should now be ready to do something exciting. This chapter will show you the fundamental principles of animation, which we will use to build the foundation for a video game. Chapter 9 will discuss how we can integrate some principles of physics into our simulations to make them more lifelike. Chapter 10 will then show you how to combine all your knowledge along with some new ideas into a fully playable game.

8.1 Animation

We can create the illusion of movement by simply drawing a shape somewhere on the screen, then erasing it and drawing it in a slightly different location. Let's demonstrate this idea by creating a small program (see Figure 8.1) that moves a ball across the screen.

The program in Figure 8.1 uses a `for`-loop to make **x** start at 1 and increment to 800 (the width of the screen). Inside the loop, a circle is drawn at the position **x,y**, where **y** has been previously set to 300 (halfway down the screen). Notice that two colors are given in the circle statement. The first is the color of the outline of the circle, and the second (which defaults to the background color if not given) is the color of the interior of the circle. A small delay has been added (10 milliseconds) and then the circle is erased by redrawing it in the background color (**white**).

```
y=300
size=20
LineWidth 3
for x = 1 to 800
   circle x,y,x+size,y+size,blue,red
   delay 10
   circle x,y,x+size,y+size,white,white
next
end
```

Figure 8.1: This program moves a ball across the screen.

8.2 Experimenting with the Program

We can learn a lot about animation by experimenting with this simple program. If you change the variable **size**, for example, you can control how big the ball is. The value of the variable **y**, controls the vertical position of the ball as it moves across the screen.

We can slow the ball's movement by increasing the amount of delay. We can speed up the ball by decreasing the delay to zero. If we want the ball to move even faster, we can increase how fast the variable **x** is changing.

In a normal for-loop, the value of the control variable is incremented by one each time the next statement is executed. If we change the for statement in Figure 8.1 to the following, then the value of **x** will increase by three each time the next is executed.

```
for x = 1 to 800 step 3
```

Experiment with the program. Try making the ball different sizes and different colors. Move the ball to different vertical positions on the screen. Speed up the ball and slow it down by changing both the delay and the step size.

Try a **size** of 20 and a `step` of 30 and see how the ball moves, and then temporarily comment out (put // at the beginning of the line) the line that erases the ball. This should help you see how the animation is taking place. Another thing that might help is to keep the erasing line, but increase the delay to something large like 500 (i.e. $\frac{1}{2}$ second). Temporarily add a second 500 ms delay following the second circle statement to help see the animation effect.

Change all occurrences of the variable **y** in Figure 8.1 to **x**. Try to guess, before you run the program, how the ball's movement will be affected by this change.

The new movement, as you will see, is a diagonal. If you study the program you should be able to see how this movement is created.

One of the things that you should have noticed, as you experimented with the program, is that there is some flicker of the ball as it moves. Faster speeds and larger balls probably cause the most flicker. It is hard to predict how your system will respond, because the type of video card and the speed of your processor will change how much flicker your system will have.

After you have finished exploring various options, return the program to its original form and add the statement `flip on` as the first line in the program and the statement `flip` as a line following the first circle statement. If you run the program after adding these two statements, you will see that it performs just like before, except that there is no flicker. Let's see why.

The reason flicker occurs is that the viewer sees graphic objects while they are being drawn. That means you sometimes see the complete object and sometimes only part of an object because the drawing is not yet completed. The RobotBASIC flip-system solves this problem.

8.3 `Flip On` and `Flip`

Normally a Window's based PC manipulates the video display by writing directly to the video memory. When a `Flip On` command is executed, RobotBASIC starts using two areas of memory – the area that is being displayed by the video hardware and a second area that is used as a buffer.

If the `flip` is turned on, any command that displays text or graphics operates on the buffer screen (which cannot be seen during printing or drawing). When a `flip` command is executed RobotBASIC tells the hardware to display the buffer memory, causing the viewer to *immediately* see the completely drawn screen.

When the `flip` is executed, something else also happens. Right after the hardware is told to start displaying the buffer, the contents of that buffer is copied to a new buffer that will be used by future output statements. The video display is simply flipping constantly between these two buffer areas. This allows a program to work exactly the same, but with `flip`, there is no flicker. This may sound complicated, so let's look at a simple example illustrate exactly how this works.

The program in Figure 8.2 dramatically demonstrates how flip eliminates the flicker that occurs when you see objects being drawn. Enter the program as shown and run it. The program draws 100 randomly chosen shapes (about half are rectangles and half are circles because about half the numbers generated by `random(100)` will be greater than 50). Each shape has random colors, a random size and is placed at a random position.

When this program is run, you see all the shapes being drawn on the screen and then there is a pause and the entire process repeats. If you remove the comments from the `flip on` and the `flip` statements, and rerun the program, you will see a huge difference. All the shapes just suddenly appear, then there is the pause, then everything repeats.

You might try changing the amount of delay to help you see what is happening.

```
// Flip on
LineWidth 4
while True
    for i = 0 to 100
        // choose a random position
        x = random(700)
        y = random(500)
        // choose a random size
        s = 10 + random(100)
        // choose random colors
        c1 = random(16)
        c2 = random(16)
        // decide randomly what shape
        if random(100)>50
           Circle x,y,x+s,y+s,c1,c2
        else
           Rectangle x,y,x+s,y+s,c1,c2
        endif
    next
    //Flip
    Delay 100
    ClearScr
wend
End
```

Figure 8.2: This program demonstrates the `flip` system.

8.4 The Beginnings of a Game

Now that we understand the basics of flicker-free animation, let's design a program that will be the basis for a game. This chapter will only set up the framework. Later chapters will add to what we create here.

For now, our objective is to have a cannon in the lower left-hand corner of the screen aimed upward at a 45-degree angle. If you click (using the mouse) on the cannon, we want it to shoot a cannonball. Additionally, we want to create a sliding power-bar above the cannon to enable the user of the program to select a power rating between 1 and 100 with the mouse. The speed of the cannonball will be proportional to the power selected.

We want to design this program using the modular techniques discussed in the last chapter. This means we will need at least three modules. They are:

MoveBall
DrawCannon
SelectPower

The **DrawCannon** subroutine will be the easiest to write. The only thing it does is draw a representation of a cannon in the lower-left corner of the screen, with the muzzle of the cannon pointing to the right with a 45° tilt. There are many ways to draw a cannon so we have a lot of freedom to be creative.

The **SelectPower** module should draw a rectangular box above the cannon. The user should be able to use the mouse to position a sliding indicator. If the slider is moved all the way to the top of the rectangular box, then the power will be 100. The bottom position should be zero. Any setting in between should be proportional to the selected position. To make it easy for the user, there should also be some numeric indication of the selected power.

The **MoveBall** module will animate the ball. The starting position of the ball should be near the end of the cannon. The ball should move at a 45° angle and the speed of the ball should be based on the power selected with the slider mentioned above.

8.5 Creating the **DrawCannon** Module

Now that we have a general description of what modules we need and what each should do, let's write each of the subroutines. We will start with easiest, the **DrawCannon** module.

As mentioned earlier, we can make the cannon look like anything we want. For this example, we are going to use some very simple ways to create a shape that looks a little like a cannon. You can always improve on this later.

Figure 8.3 shows the detail of how we are going to draw the cannon. Part **A** shows a simple rectangle. Part **B** draws a circle over the rectangle. Part **C** shows a line drawn from the center of the circle outward. This line will become the barrel of the cannon. In Part **D**, both the rectangle and the circle are drawn with the inside of the shape filled with the same color as the border. Also in Part **D**, the line representing the barrel is drawn with a very wide width to make it appear large and solid. As you can see, combining these simple shapes together creates an acceptable representation of a cannon. This illustrates an important point. Never just start programming. Always think about different ways to accomplish your goal. Every hour you spend planning can often save you many hours of debugging and rewriting code.

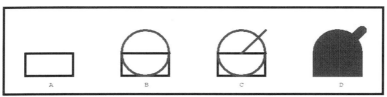

Figure 8.3: The cannon is made of three shapes.

The code to create the cannon requires only three graphic statements as shown in Figure 8.4. Since we want flicker-free animation, we will need a `flip` statement after the *group* of drawing statements (we will want all three statements executed before we flip the screen).

```
DrawCannon:
   Circle 0,500,100,600,Blue,Blue
   Rectangle 0,550,100,600,Blue,Blue
   Line 50,550,100,500,20,Blue
   Flip
Return
```

Figure 8.4: This subroutine draws the cannon.

8.6 Creating the **SelectPower** Module

Let's use the same techniques to see how the power selection slider can be built. Refer to Figure 8.5. We start by drawing a rectangle, and then we draw another one (but with a filled color, inside the first).

Part C shows how we print the word POWER at the top of the shape to tell the user what this object is and the word NUM is printed where the actual power selected will be displayed. Finally, Part D shows a third rectangle printed over the second. This third rectangle is the slider. The top of the slider will move up and down when pulled with the mouse.

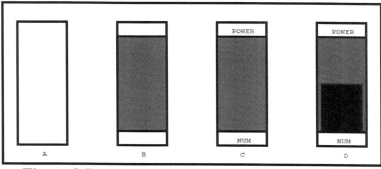

Figure 8.5: The slider is made from three rectangles.

The code to create this module is much more than just graphics statements. The reason, of course, is that we are not just drawing this diagram – the user must be able to use the mouse to select a power level. Figure 8.6 shows how to create this system.

The implementation of the power selection system requires two subroutines. This is true because parts of the graphic must be redrawn when the user selects the power level. One of the subroutines, **InitPower**, draws the initial power meter diagram. The main routine, **SelectPower**, reads the mouse and performs the actions needed to make the slider operate properly.

The **InitPower** subroutine draws two rectangles and prints the word POWER to create the graphic in Figure 8.5 B. This makes the meter appear complete as soon as it is initialized and it creates the basic form on which the selection animation can take place.

The **SelectPower** module does the real work. After the mouse information is obtained, an `if` statement checks to see if the mouse cursor is in the active area of the meter. If it is not, then the module is terminated and execution is resumed in the main program.

Another `if` statement (inside the while) ensures that the user cannot move the slider outside of the designated area.

```
SelectPower:
  ReadMouse a,b,c
  if Within(a,50,150) and Within(b,100,300)
    while c=1
      if within(b,100,300)
        Rectangle 50,100,150,300,Blue,Red
        Rectangle 60,b,140,300,Blue,Blue
        power = 100-(b-100)/2
        xystring 90,310, power,"   "
        flip
      endif
      ReadMouse a,b,c
    wend
  endif
Return

InitPower:
  Rectangle 50,70,150,330,BLue
  Rectangle 50,100,150,300,Blue,Red
  xyString 80,80,"POWER"
Return
```

Figure 8.6: This code provides for the selection of power.

8.7 Using the Mouse to Select the Power

Just having the mouse in the active area is not enough. A `while` statement continually performs the following operations as long as the left mouse button is pressed. An `if` statement makes sure the mouse is still within the expected limits, and if it is, then a RED rectangle is drawn. This rectangle (which was also drawn in the **InitPower** subroutine) effectively erases any previously selected position. A BLUE rectangle (the slider) is then drawn. It starts at the same bottom position, but its top is drawn at the current mouse position (indicated by the variable **b**). This means that moving the mouse in the slider area (with the left button pressed) will change the size of the blue rectangle (slider). When you run the program (we will do this soon) and see the slider in action, the code will make more sense.

8.8 Calculating a Numeric Power Level

The vertical position of the bottom of this rectangle is always 300 and the top (specified by the variable **b**) can range from 300 to 100. This means that the expression `b-100` will always be a number between 200 and 0. If we divide it by 2, giving `(b-100)/2`, we will get a number between 100 and 0, which is the range we want for our power level (0 to 100%). Unfortunately, the number 100 is obtained when the mouse is at the bottom of the meter, and the number 0 is obtained when the mouse is at the top. This is exactly the opposite of what we want. We can reverse this number by subtracting the previous expression from 100. The above discussion explains how the value for the variable **Power** is calculated.

The next line in the subroutine prints the value calculated in the box at the bottom of the meter. It also prints a trailing space (actually two spaces). This makes sure that any previous number is erased. Let's see how this works and why it is needed.

8.9 Fixing a Potential Error

Suppose the user has currently moved the mouse to select a power rating of 10. If they move the mouse down slightly the power will become 9. If the 9 is printed though, it will overwrite the 1, but leave the 0 (from the number 10). This would make the new value of 9 look like 90. Printing the trailing space ensures that the 0 will always be erased. This also solves a similar problem when the power level moves from 100 to 99. If we want to make sure the worst-case situation (going from 100 to a single digit power) is handled, we should print two trailing spaces.

8.10 Developing Problem-Solving Skills

Recognizing problems like the one just described and designing an appropriate solution requires creativity and problem solving skills. Your ability to deal with such problems will improve as you get more experience. Reading other people's code and studying how they solved problems is an excellent way of learning about programming.

Let's continue with our discussion of Figure 8.6. After the new meter position is drawn, a `flip` is executed to make the completed meter appear on the screen (without flicker). The mouse data is read again (we must keep reading it inside the loop and keep moving the meter until the user releases the mouse button). The loop terminates if the button is released.

8.11 Moving the Cannon Ball

The only complicated routine left for us to write is the **MoveBall** routine, which is shown in Figure 8.7. This routine is easily the most complicated routine in the book so far. If it gets too complicated for you, just try to grasp *what* this routine does instead of getting too bogged down in *how* it does its job. After you have read the entire chapter, and worked some of the exercises, go back and read this section again. If you still have trouble just move on to the next chapter. At the end of each new chapter though, as you learn more, come back to sections that gave you trouble and with your new knowledge, you may find that they don't seem as complicated. Programming is challenging, which is why it can be so much fun. It takes time though, to develop the mental skills you will need, so don't be discouraged if you don't understand everything the first time you see it.

8.12 Keeping Track of Variables

If you look at the top of Figure 8.7 you will see a number of comment statements that are not required, but are recommended as your programs increase in complexity. The comments in this example specify things that might be obvious while you are writing a program, but may not be so obvious if you come back to the program (perhaps to modify it) sometime in the future.

From the comments in Figure 8.7, you know that the variable **size** is used to specify how big the cannon ball is. The variables **xs** and **ys** represent the starting position of the ball. The ball will be moved by adjusting its current position using **dx** and **dy** as well as the current power setting. You also are told what variables are used to store temporary values. In some cases, the use of temporary values could have been eliminated. They are used here, to hold a partial calculation, because doing so can make it easier to understand the overall operation of the program, especially for beginners.

Let's look at the main part of the subroutine to see how it accomplishes its goal of moving the cannon ball.

```
MoveBall:
    //assumes the following
    // size is the size of the ball
    // xs,ys is the starting point
    // dx and dy are the increments
    // MB and S are temporary variables
    // incX and incY are temporary variables
    // x and y are temporary variables
    x = xs
    y = ys
    S=size/2
    while x<800 and y>0
        circle x-S,y-S,x+S,y+S,Black,Black
        Flip
        delay 10
        circle x-S,y-S,x+S,y+S,White,White
        incX=dx*power/20.0
        incY=dy*power/20.0
        if incX<1 then incX=1
        if incY<1 then incY=1
        x=x+incX
        y=y-incY
    wend
    Flip
Return
```

Figure 8.7: This routine moves the cannon ball.

8.13 Details of Moving the Ball

The action is to divide **size** by 2 and then store the result in the variable **S**. Then, we copy the starting values **xs** and **ys** into the variables **x** and **y** which will control where the ball is actually drawn. If we use **S** to specify the coordinates of the rectangle holding the ball, it is easy to make the position **x,y** the center of the rectangle instead of the upper-left corner as we have done in past examples (see the arguments used for `circle`.

Next, we enter a loop that will continue as long as the ball does not go off the top or right side of the screen (which means both **x** *and* **y** must have values that are on the screen). Inside this loop, we first draw the ball at the current **x,y** position and execute a `flip` to make the ball appear. Next we execute a short delay just to make sure the ball is not too fast even on very fast computers. Then we erase the ball. Notice, we do not do another `flip`, which means we won't see the ball being erased. In fact, we won't see a new ball again until it is redrawn (on the next pass through this loop). Since we only fully drawn balls at appropriate positions, we have no flicker.

Before we can restart the loop though, we have to change the values for **x** and **y** from their current values to some new values that represent the new position of the ball. If we only increment the value of **x**, then the ball will move horizontally. Similarly, if we only increment the value of **y**, then the ball will move vertically. In our case, since we want the ball to move at a 45° angle, we will want both **x** and **y** to change by the same amount. As stated earlier, the amount of change for both **x** and **y** are assumed to be stored in the variables **dx** and **dy**. We will see how this can be useful later. For now, let's assume that the values for both **dx** and **dy** are 1.

We could just add **dx** to **x** and *subtract* **dy** from **y** (because we need to *decrease* the current value of **y** to make the ball move *upward*), but this would make the ball always move at the same speed. We would like the power selected by the user to control the speed.

In order to achieve the above action, we need to calculate the actual changes we need to make for both **x** and **y**. These incremental changes for **x** and **y** will be stored in the temporary variables **incX** and **incY**. These values will be formed by multiplying **dx** and **dy** by the power level (*effectively* using the power level to choose a percentage of the maximum movement). This means that changing the power level will create larger or smaller values for **incX** and **incY** and when **x** and **y** are changed by these amounts the ball will appear to change speeds. If you try it this way though, you will see that the upper speeds don't look right because the new ball position is too far from its previous position (the ball is moving too far on each movement). A little experimentation showed that a reasonable movement could be obtained by dividing the calculations for **incX** and **incY** by 20.

In fact, we must divide by 20.0 instead of 20. If all the numbers in a calculation are integers, RobotBASIC will automatically convert the answer to an integer. Such rounding in this situation would cause many different power levels to produce the same results. This is prevented by simply making sure one of the numbers (20.0) has a floating-point value.

Two `if` statements check to make sure **incX** and **incY** are not less than one. If they are, the values are set to one. This makes sure the cannon ball will always move with some minimum power.

Once the incremental values have been calculated, we need to change the actual values of **x** and **y** by these amounts. We do this using the following two lines:

```
x = x+incX
y = y-incY
```

Notice we add the **x** value but subtract the **y** value. As mentioned earlier, this is because we must increase **x** to make the ball move to the right, but we must decrease **y** to make the ball move upward because (0,0) is the upper left corner.

When the `while`-loop repeats, the ball will be redrawn (and then erased) at the newly calculated position causing the ball to appear to move upward and across the screen. This movement continues as long as the ball is on the screen (**x** is less than 800 *and* **y** is greater than 0).

8.14 Putting It All Together

We still need an **Initialization** routine and a **MainProgram**. These are shown in Figure 8.9. Type them in followed by the code in figures 8.4, 8.6 and 8.7.

Let's see how the complete program operates. Look first at the code for the **MainProgram** in Figure 8.8. Notice how small it is. Since we have delegated all the work to other subroutines we can easily see the big picture.

The first thing the main program does is call an initialization subroutine to do any necessary preparation (more on this later). Then, a loop continually calls **SelectPower** to see if the user wants to change the setting and then on to **MoveBall** (which effectively fires the cannon). Notice that **MoveBall** is called only if the user clicks the mouse in the lower-right corner of the screen (which is where the cannon was drawn). From the user's point-of-view, this means that the cannon will fire when it is clicked with the mouse.

Notice that the check to see if the user wants to fire the cannon is made in the main program while the check to see if the user wants to move the slider is made inside the subroutine itself. This is an example of how there is no *right-way* to program. Both of these decisions could have been made the alternate way and the program would still work fine.

Writing a program is a lot like writing a story. If you gave two people the same plot line and character descriptions for writing a story, the two people would write different stories. The events in the stories might be the same (after all you gave them the same plot) but the way they tell the story will be different, because each person will tell it his or her way.

Writing a program is the same. Two people may be asked to write programs that perform some specific task, and the output from the programs might even be identical. The two programs though will be internally different because each person will handle the problem in their own way.

Every programmer will have her/his own style, but that does not mean you cannot improve your style. Take every chance you get to read and study the programs written by others. Learn from the techniques and principles you see just as an author might learn new techniques by reading the stories of others.

8.15 Running the Program

When you run the Cannon Program described in this chapter you will see the cannon drawn in the lower-left corner and the power selection meter drawn above it.

If you press the left mouse button near the middle of the power selection meter you will be able to move the slider up and down causing the meter reading (at the bottom of the meter) to change. When you get the power reading you want, just release the mouse button.

```
MainProgram:
  gosub Initialization
  while True
    gosub SelectPower
    ReadMouse a,b,c
    if c=1 and b>500 and a<100 then gosub MoveBall
  wend
end

Initialization:
  xs=120
  ys=480
  dx=1
  dy=1
  size=10
  power = 1
  flip on
  xyString 20,35,"Choose Power with"
  xyString 20,50,"    the mouse"
  xyString 10,445,"Click Cannon"
  xyString 10,460," to fire"
  LineWidth 5
  gosub InitPower
  gosub DrawCannon
  flip
Return
```

Figure 8.8: This **MainProgram** acts as the manager.

Move the mouse over the cannon and click the left button. The cannon will fire, and the ball will move diagonally up and across the screen. The speed of the ball will be based on the power level selected. Notice that you cannot select a new power while the ball is moving, because that portion of the code is not executing. Notice also that the ball moves in a straight line. Later chapters will modify the ball's movement to make it more realistic. For now though, let's enhance the program in a different way.

8.16 Adding Sound

The cannon would be more realistic if we could hear the shot. RobotBASIC makes it easy to do this.

Microsoft Window's Operating System comes with a file called **FireCannon.wav**. A **wav** file contains the information needed to create a particular sound. You could search your computer to find **FireCannon.wav** but a copy of it is included in the zip file you downloaded from our web page as the package for this book. The important thing is that we need to have this file in the same directory where the cannon program is saved.

Once that is done, you can play the sound using the following command. Notice, you do *not* include the **wav** ending with this statement.

```
PlayWav "FireCannon"
```

Insert the above line into your **MoveBall** subroutine, right before the `while`-loop. Now run the program and click the cannon. When it fires, you will hear the cannon as the ball starts to move. If you hear a *ding* instead of a cannon shot, it means RobotBASIC could not find the **FireCannon.wav** file. Check your spelling and verify the file is in the same directory where you save the program. You can also put the complete path in the `PlayWav` statement so that the file can be placed anywhere on your computer.

8.17 Muzzle Flash

We can make the cannon fire even more realistically by adding a muzzle flash. Add the subroutine shown in Figure 8.9 to your program. Add also a `gosub Fire` statement immediately following the `PlayWav` statement added earlier. Run the program again and notice the quick flash right before the cannonball is launched.

```
Fire:
   for t = 17 to 3 step -2
      circle xs-t,ys-t,xs+t,ys+t,red,red
      flip
      delay 5
      dircle xs-t,ys-t,xs+t,ys+t,white,white
   next
   flip
return
```

Figure 8.9: This subroutine can add a muzzle flash.

The **Fire** subroutine shown in Figure 8.9 creates a red flash at the end of the cannon to simulate fire protruding from the gun upon firing. The effect is easy to implement. A `for`-loop simply draws a red circle at the end of the barrel. This circle shrinks as the loop proceeds. Notice that each time through the loop the circle is drawn and then erased. This is necessary because drawing a smaller circle would not erase the larger one. The last `flip` statement in the loop makes sure the last circle is erased before returning.

8.18 Summary

In this chapter you have learned:

- The basic principles of computer animation.
- How to change the speed and direction of animation.
- How RobotBASIC's flip system can eliminate flicker.
- How to draw objects such as a cannon.
- How to create an interactive meter that allows the user to specify a parameter.
- How mathematics helps solve many programming situations.

❑   How animations can be made more realistic.

8.19 Exercises

Before moving on to the next chapter, test your knowledge and skill by trying the following exercises. Give each problem your best effort before reviewing the answers given in Appendix A.

1. Modify the program shown by Figure 8.1 so the ball moves diagonally from the lower-left corner upward and to the right. Try different sizes and different colors. Vary the speed of the ball's movement.

2. Draw the cannon so that the barrel of the gun and the bottom half of the cannon are both different colors from the rest of the cannon.

> 🖩 **Hint:** Consider altering the order that the shapes are drawn as part of your solution. Explain your answer.

3. Modify the cannon program so that the cannonball moves horizontally across the screen instead of diagonally. Once you have the ball movement working, modify the cannon barrel so that it looks like it should fire horizontally. You will also have to change the starting position of the ball.

4. Change the sound made when the cannon fires. Search your computer to find the wav files stored on it (Windows provides many wav files) or use some of the wav files included with your RobotBASIC download.

Chapter 9

Physics

In Chapter 8 you learned enough about animation and sound to create the beginnings of a game. This chapter will examine some principles of physics that will enable us to make the final game much more realistic.

When the cannon in the last chapter fired the ball, it traveled away at a fixed speed and never fell back toward the ground. This is a very unrealistic movement. We need to take the effects of gravity in consideration to make the cannonball's trajectory simulate more realistically what a real cannonball's path through the air would look like.

9.1 A Bouncing Ball

In order to examine gravity, let's write a simple program to simulate a bouncing ball. The program is shown in Figure 9.1. If you have studied the previous chapters, this program should be easy to follow.

The main program is a `while`-loop that repeats forever. Inside that loop you will find two `for`-loops. The first `for` makes the ball fall downward and the second makes it bounce upward (using the animation techniques from Chapter 8).

Enter and run the program. You should see the ball bouncing continuously on the screen, but the bouncing is unnatural, especially at the top and bottom of the bounce.

The reason of course, is that real balls don't bounce at the same speed throughout their movement.

```
x = 30
flip on
while true
  for y = 300 to 580
    circle x,y,x+20,y+20,red,black
    flip
    circle x,y,x+20,y+20,white,white
  next
  for y = 580 to 300
    circle x,y,x+20,y+20,red,black
    flip
    circle x,y,x+20,y+20,white,white
  next
wend
end
```

Figure 9.1: This program produces an unnatural bounce.

If you were to release a real ball, you would see the ball pick up speed as it falls. When it strikes the ground, the ball should bounce upward at nearly the same speed that it had before the impact (less elastic balls will loose more speed). As the ball travels higher it will slow down and eventually stop and change directions. Let's see how gravity creates this motion.

9.2 Gravity

If you take a Physics class you can learn a lot more about gravity than this book will tell you. Fortunately, we don't need to know every detail about gravity to simulate it in our programs. All we need is a basic understanding and a simplified mathematical model.

For our purposes, we can assume that gravity creates a force that pulls objects toward the earth. Imagine if you tried to push a car using a constant force (perhaps as hard as you can push). It would move very slowly at first, but if you keep pushing, the speed would increase over time. Of course, eventually you would get the car moving as fast as you can push it (its maximum or terminal speed).

The same thing happens with gravity. If you drop a ball, gravity keeps pulling it toward the ground. This constant force keeps increasing the speed of the ball until it reaches its maximum speed (which would be based on things like the amount of force the gravity exerts and the amount of friction due to the air).

If we want to be really accurate, we would have to know the exact force that gravity is exerting (the earth exerts more force than the moon, for example), how far the ball will fall (if it does not fall a reasonable distance, it won't have time to reach its maximum speed – just like you and the car if you did not push it very far) and how much friction the ball has with the air. Fortunately, we don't need to be accurate.

We are not trying to predict the exact speed or position of a real ball. We just want to make our simulated ball act a little more realistic. This means we can forget about exact numbers (the ball bouncing on the screen does not have to do it at the same speed as one in the real world) and we can just forget about maximum speeds (because we will always assume our ball is not moving over long distances) and if we want to consider friction or the elasticity of the ball, we can use any factor that makes the ball's movement seem realistic to us.

This may sound complicated, but as you will soon see, we can create a realistic model of a bouncing ball with very little effort. Refer back to Figure 9.1 and think about how you would describe the speed of the ball. In our simulated world, we are not talking about feet per second or miles per hour – we can describe the speed of our ball by specifying the number of pixels it moves each pass through the loop.

We can double the speed of the bouncing ball if we just put a `step 2` at the end of each `for` statements. We could make the ball move even faster by using `step 4` or even `6`.

> ☑ **Note:** RobotBASIC is smart enough to know when a loop must step backwards, so if you happen to use a `step 2` when you really need a `step -2` the loop will perform properly anyway.

Try making these changes with `step` to Figure 9.1 and see how the speed of the ball changes.

It is important to realize that it is reasonable for us to think of the speed of the bouncing ball in terms of the number of pixels it moves during each movement period (such as each time through a loop). The more pixels it moves, the faster the speed. Now that we understand how the speed of the ball can be simulated, let's see how gravity can affect that speed.

Remember, we said earlier that the force of gravity continually increases the speed of a falling object. Let's rewrite the program in Figure 9.1 using this idea.

Instead of using a `for`-loop to move the ball, let's just add a number **s** (a variable representing the ball's current speed) to its current position. For example, if the ball was currently at a **y** position of 100 and it had a speed of 6, then its new position would be 100+6 (or 100-6 if the ball was moving the other direction). Notice that this would basically be the same thing as using a `step` of 6 with our loops. This new method though, gives us the ability to change the speed *while* the ball is bouncing – all we have to do is change the value of **s**.

If we want to create the effects of gravity, all we have to do is *increase* (or *decrease* if the ball is moving upward) the speed by some amount every time we move the ball.

> ☑ **Note:** If the ball is going upward, against gravity, we would have to *decrease* the speed by some amount. This may seem pretty simple, and it is. This is the whole basis for adding the effect of gravity to the bouncing ball.

If we wanted to accurately simulate gravity on the moon or gravity on the earth, for example, we would have to know exactly how many feet each pixel on our screen represents, and then calculate the proper change in speed for the situation we want to simulate. In our case though, we just need to pick some number to represent the force of gravity, and then increase it or decrease it until the movement of the ball looks realistic enough. After all, it is just a game. We don't care if the simulation is accurate. We just want it to appear reasonably realistic to the user.

Another thing our program needs to do is to change the direction of the ball when it hits the ground, and change it again when it reaches the top of its bounce (when the speed has been reduced to zero). The program in Figure 9.2 shows how this can be achieved. Read the above discussion of what the program has to do, and then read the program, paying particular attention to the comments. With a little study, you should be able to see exactly how the program creates a bouncing ball complete with the effects of gravity.

Enter and run the program shown in Figure 9.2 and you will see a very realistic simulation of a bouncing ball. In order to show how realistic this simulation is, let's perform some experiments.

```
x = 30    // horizontal position of the ball
y = 300   // vertical position of the ball
          // initialized to the starting position
s = 0     // speed of ball initialized to zero
g = .1    // our guess for the force of gravity

flip on
while true
   circle x,y,x+20,y+20,red,black // draw ball
   flip
   circle x,y,x+20,y+20,white,white // erase ball
   y = y+s // calculate the new ball position
   s = s+g // calculate the new speed
   // now reverse the ball if it hits the ground
   // by making the speed negative
   if y>580 then s= -s
   // and reverse if the ball has reached the top
   // which means the speed has been negative and
   // becomes zero or positive
   // hmmmmm... if it becomes positive, then the
   // speed has been reversed... so we don't have
   // to do anything, the speed will reverse at
   // the top, all by itself
wend
end
```

Figure 9.2: Now the ball bounces with gravity.

9.3 Experimenting with the Simulation

First, let's see how the ball's movement will be affected by different amounts of gravity. Increase the value of **g** (to perhaps .2 or .3) and watch how the ball bounces faster. Decrease the value of **g** to .05 and watch the ball bounces slower. Notice the ball still bounces the same height; it just bounces faster or slower. This is what would happen if we compared a ball bouncing on the earth to one bouncing on the moon.

Imagine what would happen to a real ball if, instead of dropping the ball, you threw it at the ground. The ball would bounce higher than the point you through it from. We can simulate throwing the ball by giving it an initial speed, such as 5. Change the initial value of **s** from 0 to 5 and run the program to see the ball bounce higher than its initial starting point. Change **s** to 10 and you will see the ball bounce completely off the screen.

9.4 Changing the Elasticity

A very elastic ball (such as a super ball) will bounce almost as high as the point you drop it from, but most balls don't do as well. The ball in our simulation is perfect, in that it continues to bounce forever.

A real ball might only have 80% of its speed when it changes direction from hitting the ground. We can simulate this by changing the line

```
        if y>580 then s= -s
```
        to
```
        if y>580 then s= -s*.8
```

If you make the above changes the ball will bounce and slow down over time. If you try different values of elasticity such as .7 or .9 though the ball does not seem to respond properly.

For some values of elasticity, the ball will never stop at the bottom. Instead, it just seems to vibrate on the ground. The ball might also just quit bouncing after one or two bounces instead of steadily slowing down like a real ball. If we were using a full mathematical simulation we would not have these problems, but our simplified model does not perform exactly as expected. Luckily, it turns out we can solve both of these problems by not letting the ball go past the ground when it gets to the bottom of its travel. This could happen in our simplified model, for example, if the ball moving at a speed of 8 is at position 579 (just above the expected bottom position of 580). The new position would be 579+8 or 587, which puts some of the ball (diameter 20) below the ground (the bottom of the ball would be 587+20 or 607, but the ground is at 600). If all this seems complicated, just realize you don't really have to totally understand it. Just accept the fact that our simulation will work without problems if we just make sure the ball does not go below the ground level. We can do that by replacing the `if` statement above with the following lines:

```
if y>580
    y=581   //don't let it go too far
    s= -s*.8 //reverse and slow down
endif
```

If you make this change and run the program the ball will bounce and eventually stop, just like a real ball. If you change the ball's elasticity from .8 to .9 (making it more like a super ball, the bouncing will take a longer time to die out. If you lower the elasticity to .7 or .6 the ball will stop quicker. Try making these changes and observe the effects.

9.5 Adding Wind

A wind blowing (let's assume) from left to right would move the ball to the right. Let's see how we can simulate such a wind. First, just to make sure you are starting with a working program, make the `if-endif` change suggested above with an elasticity of .8. If the program is working correctly, the ball should bounce about ten times and stop.

Once you have the program working we can add the effects of wind by adding the following line at the beginning of the program. (Notice this could also be simulating the ball being thrown to the right initially.)

```
wind = 1
```

Also, add the following line immediately after the `while` statement.

```
x = x + wind
```

Run the program and you will see the ball being "blown" across the screen as it bounces. Even when the ball stops, the wind keeps it rolling until it goes off the right side of the screen. You can, for example, make the wind weaker (.5) or stronger (2). Figure 9.3 shows how the ball reacts

with a wind of 1 and an elasticity of .8. This figure was
created by placing a comment indicator (//) at the beginning
of the line that erases the ball.

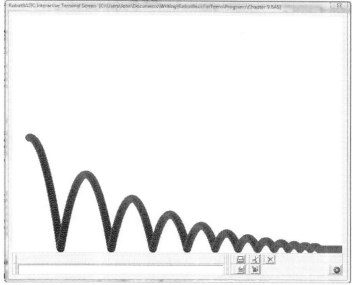

Figure 9.3: A wind-blown, bouncing ball.

Our simulation is now starting to act like a real ball.
Imagine dropping a beanbag on the floor. It might bounce
a little, but not much. Set the elasticity to something small,
perhaps 0.2 and run the program. Try it again with the
wind set to zero.

9.6 The Power of Simulation
Large companies use simulations all the time to save time
and money. Accurate simulations based on mathematical
models can help an automobile manufacturer design cars
with less wind resistance and less vibration but without
actually building the cars. NASA can determine how much

fuel would be needed to fly to Mars, without building the space ship.

RobotBASIC is a good example of a robot simulation system. It allows you to test programming ideas without actually building a robot. Think about how much easier it would be to build a robot if you could determine what sensors it would need and how those sensors should be used before you actually started construction. RobotBASIC is not just a simulation system. It is capable of controlling real-world robots too, but we will discuss that in more detail later.

The point is that simulations are valuable tools and what you have learned here is only a small sample of what can be done with the right software.

9.7 Adding Gravity to the Cannon

Now that you have an understanding of how forces such as gravity can be modeled by software, let's add gravity to the cannon project discussed in Chapter 8. You may be surprised at how easy it is to implement this concept now that we understand the principles. Figure 9.4 shows the old **MoveBall** subroutine from Chapter 8, with a few modifications (the new or modified lines are shown in bold).

The first bold line sets the amount of gravity we want our simulated world to have (in this case 0.1). The second line sets the initial value of the amount of **fall** the ball has to zero. (This just represents the speed of the ball.) A positive value here, for example, could imply the ball has been thrown downward. Similarly, a negative value could mean the ball was initially thrown upward.

Near the end of the routine you will see a change to how the ball's vertical position (**y**) is calculated. The change is that the value of **fall** (the amount of extra drop due to gravity) is added to the current value of **y**. Notice that the value of **incY** is trying to move the ball upward, while the value of **fall** is trying to move it downward. Initially, the ball will move upward (because **fall** is zero), but over time, the force of gravity keeps increasing the ball's downward speed (its **fall**) causing it to drop back to the ground.

```
MoveBall:
    //assumes the following
    // size is the size of the ball
    // xs,ys is the starting point
    // dx and dy are the increments
    // MB and S are temporary variables
    // incX and incY are temporary
variables
    // x and y are temporary variables
    gravity = .1
    fall = 0
    x = xs
    y = ys
    S=size/2
    PlayWav "FireCannon"
    gosub Fire
    while x<800 and y<600
        circle x-S,y-S,x+S,y+S,Black,Black
        flip
        delay 10
        circle x-S,y-S,x+S,y+S,White,White
        incX=dx*power/20.0
        incY=dy*power/20.0
        if incX<1 then incX=1
        if incY>1 then incY=1
        x=x+incX
        y=y-incY+fall
        fall = fall + gravity
    wend
    repeat
      ReadMouse a,b,c
    until c=0
    Flip
return
```

Figure 9.4: These few changes add gravity to the cannon.

The next line in the program calculates the new value for **fall**. If you understood the discussions of gravity in this chapter, then this calculation should be easy to follow. Our simplified model simply means the amount of **fall** for any time period will increase by the amount of gravity we have.

The only other change made to Figure 9.3 is to the `while`. Without gravity, the ball could theoretically exit the screen on the right side or the top. With gravity, the ball could still exit on the right side, but a low-power shot will drop off the bottom of the screen. The change to the `while` reflects this new condition for terminating the loop.

9.8 Summary
In this chapter you have learned:
- ❑ How to simulate real-world forces such as wind and gravity.
- ❑ How to create a bouncing ball with adjustable elasticity.
- ❑ How a ball will react to different levels of gravity.
- ❑ Why simulations are important.

9.9 Exercises
Before moving on to the next chapter, test your knowledge and skill by trying the following exercises. Give each problem your best effort before reviewing the answers given in Appendix A.

1. Enter the programs and suggested alterations discussed in the chapter and verify that all the programs work as expected.

2. Modify the wind-blown ball so that when it hits the right side of the screen, it starts bouncing back to the left and when it gets to the left side it starts bouncing back to the right, etcetera. This is more representative of a ball being initially thrown toward a wall. Set the elasticity to 1 so that the ball will continue to bounce back and forth across the screen. The realistic motion might surprise you.

Chapter 10

A Simple Video Game

In this chapter we are going to convert the cannon program from Chapter 8 (along with the gravity modification of Section 9.7 in Chapter 9) into a complete video game. We will assume that you have the program, complete with the effects of gravity, sound, and a muzzle flash, entered and working properly.

10.1 The Game

Let's start by specifying what we want our game to do. The cannon will operate just like it did before. That is, we set the power level with the mouse, and fire the cannon by clicking it.

The first thing we want to add is something to shoot at. We will create a tank that will periodically move to a new location. Since the tank could end up on the far right side of the screen, you should modify the amount of gravity in the program to ensure that the cannon ball can be fired all the way across the screen. Make the decrease in gravity minor though, because we want full power to make the ball travel only slightly further than the screen limits.

Once we have the tank as a target, we will create an explosion when it is hit, and of course, we will need a way to keep score and start a new game.

10.2 The `DrawShape` Command

RobotBASIC has many graphic capabilities. One very useful command is `DrawShape` that allows us to specify a shape using a *string* of characters. Variables in RobotBASIC can hold integers (like 6) or floating-point numbers (such as 6.8) or strings (like "cat" or "dog5").

The shape to be drawn will be defined by the letters in the string used by `DrawShape`. Refer to the Help files for complete information on `DrawShape`. The discussion here explains only the capabilities we will use in this program.

Imagine that `DrawShape` starts by placing a pen on the screen and then moves the pen based on the letters in the string. The directions for each letter are given below.

> ✍ **Note:** Lower case letters cause movement as well as drawing. Upper case letters cause movement without drawing.

---

l – left	**r** – right
u – up	**d** – down
q – up and left	**w** – up and right
a – down and left	**s** – down and right

The letters used for up, down, left, and right are all obvious but the letters used for the diagonals are not, unless you look at the keyboard. Notice that the letters **q**, **w**, **a**, and **s** form a square on your keyboard with each letter in a corner of that square. Notice that the **q** is in the upper-left corner of the square, and the letter **q** causes movement up and left. This means, the string "**ddrruu**" would draw a U shaped object and the string "**rrrrqqaa**" would draw a triangle. The short program in Figure10.1 demonstrates a few of the capabilities of `DrawShape`. It produces the screen in Figure 10.2.

```
triangle = "rrrrqqaa"
box = "uurrddll"
diamond = "wsaq"
tank = "quwrrwqsrrsrrsdallllllll"

LineWidth 3
for scale = 1 to 5
  y=100*scale
  DrawShape triangle,100,y,scale*8,Red
  DrawShape box,300,y,scale*8,Blue
  DrawShape diamond,500,y,scale*8,Black
next

while True
  // move tank slowly to the right
  for x = 100 to 450
    DrawShape tank,x,550,8,Blue
    delay 20
    DrawShape tank,x,550,8,-1
  next
  // move smaller tank quickly to left
  for x = 450 to 100 step -3
    DrawShape tank,x,550,4,Blue
    delay 20
    DrawShape tank,x,550,4,-1
  next
wend
end
```

Figure 10.1: This program demonstrates DrawShape.

The first part of the program assigns some string values to several variables. These strings define the shapes. Trace the movements indicated by the letters on a sheet of graph paper to see how each shape is formed.

The first argument given to DrawShape is the name of the variable holding the string (or you can just provide the string in quotes without a variable if you wish).

The next two arguments are the x,y coordinates where you want the shape to start drawing. Next is a number indicating the scale to be used. Normally the movement for each letter in the string will be one pixel. If you specify a scale, it changes each movement to as many pixels as specified by the scale value. If, for example, the scale is 3, each movement specified in the string will be 3 pixels. This makes it easy to create multiple sizes from one shape definition.

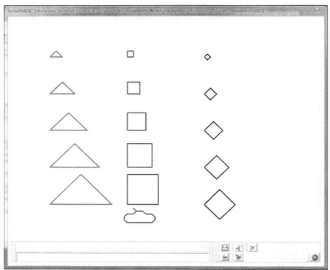

Figure 10.2: DrawShape makes it easy to create shapes of different types, sizes, and colors.

The last argument in our example specifies the color to be used for the shape. If the color is -1, then the background color is used (ideal for erasing a shape).

The first for-loop in Figure 10.1 shows how a loop can be used to control where a shape is drawn as well as what size it will be. The while-loop causes the actions of the two for-loops inside it to be repeated endlessly. The first for-loop moves the tank to the right, and the second moves it back. Notice how the tank changes sizes and speeds when it moves back.

10.3 Programming the Game

Now that you understand how shapes can be drawn, we can proceed with converting the cannon program from Chapter 8 into a game. Most of the subroutines from Chapter 8 will need some modification and we will need to write a few new ones. If you understood Chapter 8 you should have no trouble understanding how our modifications can create a game. If you have trouble understanding any aspects of this chapter, consider going back to study Chapter 8 again.

We will examine each of the routines from Chapter 8 and discuss the modifications. Many routines have only minor changes, but the routines will be repeated here for clarity. All of the new lines will be shown in **bold** to help you see how the original program was modified. The modified **Initialization** subroutine is given in Figure 10.3.

```
Initialization:
  xs=120
  ys=480
  dx=1
  dy=1
  size=10
  power = 1
  flip on
  xyString 20,35,"Choose Power with"
  xyString 20,50,"      the mouse"
  xyString 10,445,"Click Cannon"
  xyString 10,460,"      to fire"
  LineWidth 5
  gosub InitPower
  gosub DrawCannon
  flip
  gosub InitTank
return
```

Figure 10.3: This is the new Initialization routine.

The four routines **DrawCannon, SelectPower, Fire** and **InitPower** require no modifications at all and are listed again in Figure 10.4 for convenience.

The new **MoveBall** subroutine is shown in Figure 10.5. It required only minor modification. First, an `if` statement checks to see if the cannonball has hit the tank. This is true (at the time the ball hits the ground or goes off the screen) if the horizontal position of the cannonball (**x**) is close to the tank's position (**Tx**). The range used is -3 to +60. Can you explain why?

If the ball hits the tank, the variable **hit** is set to true and the explosion is created. Notice that **NumShots** is always increased by one. These variables are new to the program and indicate if the tank was hit and how many times the cannon has been fired (for scoring). More on this later.

Three totally new routines are needed. One of these initializes the tank. Another moves the tank from its current position (**Tx**) to a new random position (**tx**). The third routine creates the sound and visual (much like the muzzle flash) for an explosion when the cannonball hits the tank. These routines are shown in Figure 10.6. If you understood the discussions about `DrawShape` you should be able to understand this code.

```
DrawCannon:
  Circle 0,500,100,600,Blue,Blue
  Rectangle 0,550,100,600,Blue,Blue
  Line 50,550,100,500,20,Blue
  Flip
Return

SelectPower:
  ReadMouse a,b,c
  if Within(a,50,150) and Within(b,100,300)
    while c=1
      if within(b,100,300)
        Rectangle 50,100,150,300,Blue,Red
        Rectangle 60,b,140,300,Blue,Blue
        power = 100-(b-100)/2
        xystring 90,310, power,"   "
        flip
      endif
      ReadMouse a,b,c
    wend
  endif
Return

Fire:
  for t = 17 to 3 step -2
    circle xs-t,ys-t,xs+t,ys+t,red,red
    flip
    delay 5
    circle xs-t,ys-t,xs+t,ys+t,white,white
  next
  flip
return

InitPower:
  Rectangle 50,70,150,330,BLue
  Rectangle 50,100,150,300,Blue,Red
  xyString 80,80,"POWER"
Return
```

Figure 10.4: These routines required no modification.

```
MoveBall:
   //assumes the following
   // size is the size of the ball
   // xs,ys is the starting point
   // dx and dy are the increments
   // MB and S are temporary variables
   // incX and incY are temporary variables
   // x and y are temporary variables
   gravity = .1
   fall = 0
   x = xs
   y = ys
   S=size/2
   PlayWav "FireCannon"
   gosub Fire
   while x<800 and y<600
      circle x-S,y-S,x+S,y+S,Black,Black
      flip
      delay 10
      circle x-S,y-S,x+S,y+S,White,White
      incX=dx*power/20.0
      incY=dy*power/20.0
      if incX<1 then incX=1
      if incY<1 then incY=1
      x=x+incX
      y=y-incY+fall
      fall = fall + gravity
   wend
   Flip
   if within(x,Tx-3,Tx+60)
      hit = true
      gosub Explosion
   endif
   NumShots = NumShots+1
Return
```

Figure 10.5: This is the new **MoveBall** routine.

```
InitTank:
  tank = "quwrrwqsrrsrrsdallllllll"
  Tx = 200+Random(550)
  DrawShape tank,Tx,599,5
  gosub MoveTank
return

MoveTank:
  // Tx is the current tank location
  // move it a random distance but never less
  // than 200 nor more than 750
  // now choose a new location
  tx = 200+Random(550)
  for t = Tx to tx
     DrawShape tank,t,599,5
     flip
     DrawShape tank,t,599,5,-1
  next
  Tx = tx
  DrawShape tank,Tx,599,5
  flip
return

Explosion:
  PlayWav "Explode"
  for t = 5 to 60 step 2
     circle x-t,590-t,x+t,590+t,red,random(16)
     flip
     delay 20
  next
  for t = 60 to 3 step -2
     circle x-t,590-t,x+t,590+t,white,gray
     flip
  next
return
```

Figure 10.6: These three routines are completely new.

The only routine left for us to consider is the **MainProgram** routine. It required many modifications because it is the manager that makes all the decisions required to create the game. Refer to Figure 10.7 as you read the discussion in the next section.

```
MainProgram:
  gosub Initialization
  while True
    score = 0
    xyString 400,100,"Score = ",score,"    "
    flip
    for tries = 5 to 1
      xyString 375,150,"Tanks left = ",tries
      flip
      NumShots = 0
      hit = false
      while NumShots<2 and not hit
          gosub SelectPower
          ReadMouse a,b,c
          if c=1 and b>500 and a<100 then gosub MoveBall
      wend
      // add up score ********
      if hit and NumShots = 1 then score = score + 3
      if hit and NumShots = 2 then score = score + 1
      xyString 400,100,"Score = ",score,"    "
      flip
      if tries > 1 then gosub MoveTank
    next
    // game over
    xyString 375,150,"Tanks left = 0 "
    xyString 325,200,"Click the mouse for new game"
    flip
    repeat
      ReadMouse a,b,c
    until c=1
    gosub MoveTank
    xyString 325,200,"                            "
    flip
  wend
end
```

Figure 10.7: The new **MainProgram** routine manages the logic for creating the game (complete with scoring).

10.4 Analyzing the **MainProgram**

The **MainProgram** initializes a variable (**score**) to zero so that it can be used to keep track of the score in the game. The score and the number of tanks left are always displayed for the user.

The game allows you two tries to hit the tank before it moves to a new location (considered a new tank). This is accomplished with the `while`-loop. If you hit the tank on the first try, you get three points. Since you can use the first try to home in on the tank's position, you only get one point if you hit it on the second try. These decisions are made by two `if` statements that monitor the variables whose values are set by **MoveBall**.

The subroutine **MoveTank** is called when it is time to move the tank to a new location (after the tank is hit or you miss it twice or at the start of a new game). Notice how the "new game" message is erased by just printing spaces over it.

A detailed explanation of every line in the program has been purposely omitted. Generalized descriptions of all the changes have been provided, but at this stage in your learning, your understanding of programming will be enhanced if you force yourself to seriously study the code. If you have understood all the examples and performed all the exercises in the previous chapters, you should be able to study this program and see how everything works. If you are unsure of why a line of code is there, try commenting it out and running the program to see the results. Often this can help you see why something is needed.

Don't be discouraged if some aspects of the program require a reasonable amount of study in order to understand them. You will learn far more about programming as you struggle through such an analysis than you will just entering some example code from a book.

As you examine the code for this program, pay particular attention to how the controlling logic decides when to call the subroutines that perform the actual work that needs to be done.

This divide and conquer ideology is a powerful concept that must be used to write large programs. Without such a philosophy, complex programs can quickly become unmanageable.

Learning to become a good programmer means learning about logic, which can only be learned by exercising your mental skills. Programming is one of the best ways to boost your logical abilities. If you see it as a challenge, it can be exciting and rewarding.

10.5 Summary

In this chapter you have learned:

- ❑ How to organize the code for a computer game.
- ❑ How previously created modules can help create a new program.
- ❑ How complex actions can be broken down into independent subroutines that are called when needed (based on the logic programmed into a **MainProgram** or other control module).

10.6 Exercises

Before moving on to the next chapter, test your knowledge and skill by trying the following exercises. Give each problem your best effort before reviewing the answers given in Appendix A.

1. Enter and run the program shown in the chapter. Study exactly what happens and how the game operates so that you know what to look for when you analyze the operation of the code.

2. Study the code for the tank game making sure you understand what each line and section of code does and why it was used. Notice things such as when tank movements occur and when scores are updated. Make special note of anything that makes you wonder how it is accomplished.

3. Modify the program in some way. For example, make the tank larger or smaller (or a different shape) or allow the user more tries or more tanks or any other modification you think would be interesting. Try the program after you have made your initial changes and see if anything you did

causes problems with other aspects of the program. For example, if you make the tank larger, you will see that the cannonball will sometimes hit the tank without causing an explosion or crediting your score. You might also notice that the explosion does not always remove the entire tank from the screen. Searching through the code to make the corrections needed to make your modifications work properly can be a wonderful challenge and a superb learning experience.

Chapter 11

Writing a Paint Program

In this chapter we will design a Paint Program that allows you to draw on the screen. The program will have many features, but don't expect it to have the functionalities you might find in a commercial program.

The purpose of this chapter is not to create a professional Paint program, just as the Tank video game we developed in Chapter 10 was not the perfect game. The point is to let you *play* with something interesting and exciting while you learn about new programming ideas and concepts. Besides, once you gain more experience, you can enhance the program by coding additional functionalities and features according to your needs and wishes.

11.1 Defining the Project

The first step is to specify what we want our program to do. We will need some type of menu on the left side of the screen that allows the user to select and activate the various actions that will be required to draw on the screen using the program. These are the actions we want to implement.

The user should be able to:
- Choose a brush style from among various styles.
- Draw freehand using the mouse.
- Clear the screen with a selected color.
- Fill an area on the screen with a selected color.

- Save the current picture.
- Open a previously saved picture.
- Choose a color from among 10 active colors.
- Redefine any of the active colors to some new color. (This last feature will be implemented at the end of this chapter as an enhancement for the original program.)

Let's start with the design of the **MainProgram**. Remember, this routine does not need to do any actual work. Its purpose is to coordinate the over all actions of the program and to decide which subroutines should be called to carry out the actions. We will initially makeup names for these subroutines, and then worry about creating each of them one at a time. Figure 11.1 shows the **MainProgram**.

```
MainProgram:
  gosub Initialization
  while True
    ReadMouse a,b,c
    if a<125
      gosub ProcessMenu
    else
      gosub DrawBrush
    endif
  wend
end
```

Figure 11.1: This is the start of our Paint Program.

The **MainProgram** starts by performing some initialization and then enters an endless loop. We will need to decide exactly what initialization must be done, but certainly it should draw the menu on the left side of the screen. As we develop the other subroutines, we will know what initial conditions they require.

Inside the endless loop, the program reads the mouse data and checks to see if the mouse cursor is over the menu (we will assume the menu resides in the left 125 pixels of the screen). If the mouse is over the menu the routine calls a **ProcessMenu** subroutine that will perform the necessary actions for each choice in the menu. If the mouse is not over the menu, the **DrawBrush** subroutine is called to perform the actual drawing.

In order to design these two subroutines, we must determine exactly how they will interact. For example, the **ProcessMenu** routine will allow the user to choose things like colors and brush styles and sizes. This information will be needed by the **DrawBrush** routine, so the information will have to be stored in variables. Let's decide on the names of those variables now. The variable **co** will hold the selected color and **br** will indicate the selected brush. In RobotBASIC there are 16 standard colors numbered 0 to 15 (See the CONSTANTS help page), so **co** will be assigned one of these numbers.

For the brushes, the plan is to have two different brush styles, a solid circle and an open circle (the interior being the background color which we will store in the variable **bc**). There will be three different sizes of the solid brush but only two sizes of the open brush, because the small size will be too small to see the interior color anyway. We need a way to code the size and style into a numbering scheme (a single number representing both the size and style would be nice). The one chosen is shown in Figure 11.2.

The first column shows what the brush will look like. The second column gives the radius that we want each brush to have. The code for the solid brushes will be the radius itself. The code for the open brushes will be the radius+20. You will see shortly how we can use this coded information to make the program easier to write.

	Radius	Code
·	2	2
●	6	6
●	12	12
○	6	26
○	12	32

Figure 11.2: These are the brushes used by the Paint Program.

11.2 Drawing the Brushes

We will use a subroutine called **DrawBrush** to perform the actual drawing done by the user. The process for making this happen was introduced back in Chapter 5 (see Figure 5.2). All the subroutine has to do is keep drawing the selected brush at the current mouse position in the selected color. This causes mouse movements (with the button pressed) to leave a trail. The subroutine is shown in Figure 11.3.

The main part of the code is all inside a `while`-loop that repeats as long as the mouse button is held down. Inside the loop, an `if` statement checks to make sure the user does not try to move the mouse over the menu (we don't want them to draw there). Inside that `if`, another `if` will decide which brush to use.

Remember that all of the solid brushes use a code that is less than 20 while the other brushes have codes greater than 20 (see Figure 11.2). The `if` statement can decide which style of brush to make by checking to see if the current brush code (stored in **br**) is less than 20.

If **br** is less than 20, then we set **s** equal to **br** (just to make the `Circle` statement easy to write) and draw the circle in the same way we drew the cannonball or other circles in previous chapters. In this case, we set both the foreground and the background colors to **co** to create a solid circle.

If **br** is greater than 20, then we set **s** equal to **br-20** (because the code for these brushes is 20 bigger than the radius). When we draw the circle this time, we use **bc** for the background color.

```
DrawBrush:
  // assumes br defines the brush and
  // co is the color
  // a,b,c are already the mouse data
  while c=1
    if a>125
      if br<20
        s=br
        Circle a-s,b-s,a+s,b+s,co,co
      else
        s=(br-20)
        Circle a-s,b-s,a+s,b+s,co,bc
      endif
    endif
    ReadMouse a,b,c
  wend
return
```

Figure 11.3: This subroutine performs the actual drawing done by the program.

The last thing we do is read the mouse data again so the `while`-loop can decide when to quit. If we did not read the mouse again, the variable **c** would not change and the loop would never terminate. Notice how the codes described earlier for the brush styles made it easy to create this subroutine. Often, doing a little planning and designing before you begin to write code can save you time in the long run.

11.3 The **DrawMenu** Subroutine

The **DrawMenu** subroutine does just that; it draws the menu on the left side of the screen. It will look like Figure 11.4. The left column is 65 pixels wide and the right is 60. We could have made both columns the same width, but the text looks less crowded with a slightly wider column.

The user selects a particular action by clicking inside the appropriate box. The right column, for example, shows 10 colors, each in its own box. If you left-click the mouse inside any of these boxes, its color will become the active color. Left-clicking the mouse inside any of the boxes in the left column of the menu will allow the user to select a brush shape or perform some special actions.

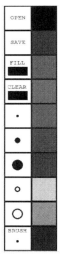

Figure 11.4: The Paint Menu

Let's examine the menu choices to make sure you know what to expect from each one. The SAVE and OPEN menu options allow the user to save the current picture and retrieve it later.

If the user clicks the FILL box, the cursor will change to a cross (+) to indicate that FILL mode is active. If the user then clicks the mouse inside some enclosed area on the drawing screen, that area will be filled with the current active color. Notice the box under the word FILL. That box (and the one under CLEAR) will always be the active color so the user is always given a visual indication of currently active color. The CLEAR option clears the entire screen using the current active.

The box at the bottom left of the menu shows the current brush style in the currently selected colors so that the user always knows what choices have been made.

Now that you know what the menu will look like, let's look at the code for drawing it. It is shown in Figure 11.5. Most of the code should be easy to follow, but there are a few places that deserve special attention.

```
DrawMenu:
  LineWidth 3
  c=0 // used to specify the color
  for i=0 to 540 step 60
     Rectangle 1,i,65,i+60,black,white
     Rectangle 65,i,125,i+60,black,c
     c=c+1
  next
  xyString 15,20,"OPEN"
  xyString 15,80,"SAVE"
  xyString 13,130,"FILL"
  xyString 8,190,"CLEAR"
  xyString 9,542,"BRUSH"
  s=2
  x=32
  y=270
  circle x-s,y-s,x+s,y+s,black,black
  s=6
  y=330
  circle x-s,y-s,x+s,y+s,black,black
  s=12
  y=390
  circle x-s,y-s,x+s,y+s,black,black
  s=6
  y=450
  circle x-s,y-s,x+s,y+s,black,white
  s=12
  y=510
  circle x-s,y-s,x+s,y+s,black,white
  gosub Now
return
```

Figure 11.5: This code draws the Paint Menu.

The code starts by using a `for`-loop to draw all the boxes for the menu. Each pass through the loop, a left box is drawn with a white interior and a right box is drawn with a color specified by the variable **c** (which is incremented on each pass through the `for`-loop).

The next portion of the code prints the appropriate text at the proper places on the menu. Next, a series of `Circle` statements draw the brushes. Finally, the current brush style and color is drawn by a subroutine called **Now** (the brush that is in use *now*).

Let's see how to write the **Now** subroutine. It is shown in Figure 11.6. It starts by updating the two rectangles in the CLEAR and FILL options. Then it erases the old brush and draws the new brush using similar code to what we saw earlier in the **DrawBrush** subroutine. This subroutine should be called every time a new color or brush is selected. Can you explain why?

```
Now:
  Rectangle 10,150,55,170,co,co
  Rectangle 10,210,55,230,co,co
  a=32
  b=577
  s=12
  // first erase the old brush
  Circle a-s,b-s,a+s,b+s,white,white
  if br<20
    s=br
    Circle a-s,b-s,a+s,b+s,co,co
  else
    s=(br-20)
    circle a-s,b-s,a+s,b+s,co,bc
  endif
return
```

Figure 11.6: This subroutine updates the menu to the current choices.

There are only two routines left to write. The most complicated one is the **ProcessMenu** module, so let's look at it first. This subroutine does a lot of work. It is responsible for determining what the user wants to do and performing the actions necessary to handle the request. Since there are many small actions, the code is broken down into small sections that perform specific functions. This makes the routine easy to write and understand.

11.4 The ProcessMenu Subroutine

The code in **ProcessMenu** (Figure 11.7) begins by getting the latest mouse data to ensure the user is trying to select an option. If the mouse cursor is not over the menu or a button is not pressed, then the program simply returns instead of continuing to process the menu.

If the cursor is over the color choices in the menu, then the variable holding the current color (**co**) is set to **b**/60. This formula is an integer division and results in the number 0 for the top color, the number 1 for the next color down, the number 2 for the third one and so forth. Notice how the use of a mathematical formula here eliminates the need for 10 different if statements for checking to see if the mouse is over one of the 10 colors (see how if statements are used below to determine which menu option was selected).

If the cursor was not over the colors, then it has to be over the left-side options (because if it had not been over the menu the program would have returned earlier). Each of these options is handled individually.

There are five if statements that check to see if the user has clicked one of the brushes. If they have, the variable **br** is set to the appropriate brush code.

The next if statement in Figure 11.7 processes the CLEAR option. It clears the screen to the current color and then redraws the menu. This redrawing is necessary because the `ClearScr` command clears the entire screen (thus erasing the menu).

```
ProcessMenu:
  ReadMouse a,b,c
  if a>125 or c=0 then return
  if within(a,60,125)
    if c=1 then co = b/60 // process color
  else // other menu item
    if within(b,240,300) then br=2
    if within(b,300,360) then br=6
    if within(b,360,420) then br=12
    if within(b,420,480) then br=26
    if within(b,480,540) then br=32
    if within(b,180,240)
      bc = co
      clearscr bc
      gosub DrawMenu
    endif
    if within(b,120,180)
      SetCursor -3
      repeat
        ReadMouse a,b,c
      until c=0
      repeat
        ReadMouse a,b,c
      until c=1
      if a>125 then FloodFill a,b,co
      SetCursor
    endif
    if within(b,60,120)
      Input "SAVING: Enter a File Name",filename
      if filename<>"" then WriteScr filename
    endif
    if within(b,0,60)
      Input "OPENING: Enter a File Name",filename
      if filename<>"" then ReadScr filename
      gosub DrawMenu
    endif
  endif
  gosub Now
return
```

Figure 11.7: This code processes the menu options.

Another `if` statement checks to see if the FILL option has been chosen. If it has, the cursor is changed (as mentioned earlier) using the `SetCursor` command and then a `repeat-until` loop is used to wait for the user to release the left mouse button. Another `repeat-until` loop waits until the user presses the left mouse button. When they do, the `FloodFill` command is used to fill the area specified by the mouse position with the current active color. Finally, the cursor is set back to its default style. See the help files if you want to learn more about the `SetCursor` and `FloodFill` commands.

An `if` statement checks to see if the user has selected the SAVE box to save the current drawing to a file on disk. If so, the user is prompted to enter a name for the file. The entire screen will be saved in this file using the `WriteScreen` command and later retrieved using the OPEN option.

Another `if` statement checks to see if the OPEN box has been selected. If so, the user is prompted to enter a file name which should be the same as a previously saved file. The routine then restores the entire screen from this file using the `ReadScreen` command and then the **DrawMenu** routine is called (can you explain why?).

Note: Our SAVE and OPEN routines ignore the request if the user does not enter a name by just pressing ENTER, but it does not check for any other errors. This means the program may crash or act unpredictably if the user misspells the file name. Detailed error checking is beyond the scope of this introductory book, but you can refer to the help files for more information on this important topic.

11.5 Initialization

The code to perform the initialization is shown in Figure 11.8. Now that we have written all the routines, it is easy to determine what items need to be initialized. The module simply establishes the default values for the color, the brush, and the background color, and then draws the menu.

```
Initialization:
  co = 0
  br = 2
  bc = white
  gosub DrawMenu
return
```

Figure 11.8: The Initialization Subroutine.

11.6 Putting it all Together

Enter the routines in Figures 11.1 and 11.3 to 11.8 to create the Paint program then run it and try drawing some shapes. Remember to make sure that the **MainProgram** routine is the topmost routine. Figure 11.9 shows some sample "artwork" created with our Paint Program.

Figure 11.9: Even though our Paint Program is simple, you can still use it to draw interesting things.

The Paint Program demonstrates a lot of techniques and programming principles. It is important however, that you understand that you are just beginning to explore the power of programming. If you read through the help pages for RobotBASIC you will find hundreds of commands that have not even been mentioned in this book. Once you understand the basic principles of programming though, you should be able to use any of these commands if you are willing to read and study. Before sending you off on your own, though, we will make a modification to our Paint Program to give you a glimpse of some of the power that awaits you.

11.7 Array Variables

One of the most powerful capabilities of a computer language is array-variables. With the *simple* variables we have used throughout this book, you have to give a unique name to each variable. With an array variable you create one name that refers to a *list* of variables and then use an *index* number to tell the computer which one (in the list) you want to use. Each item in the array is called an *element*. The first thing that must be done is to create the array. We can create an array called **MyNums** with space for 20 items like this.

```
Dim MyNums[20]
```

The 20 elements are numbered 0 through 19 and can be accessed as shown in the following example. Notice that the index that specifies the element to be used is surrounded by [ ] (brackets).

```
MyNums[2] = 6
MyNums[1] = 12
MyNums[0] = MyNums[3] + 14
for a = 0 to 2
      Print MyNums[a]
next
```

This example demonstrates several details. The first and second lines show how to store numbers into elements of the array. The third line shows that an array reference can be used on either side of the equals sign. The `for`-loop shows one reason why arrays can be such a powerful tool.

The `for`-loop causes **a** to be 0 the first time through the loop, then 1 and finally 2. Notice this means that the single

Print statement will print all three of the elements used in the program. If you are thinking that it would still take three lines of code to do this printing, then imagine how this helps if you want to print an array of 100 or even 1000 elements. (Both of these situations would still only take 3 lines of code.)

Learning all the ways arrays can be used would take far more space than is available in this book, but let's modify our Paint Program to demonstrate how the power of arrays can make programming far more efficient. Let's first look at a simple example to make sure you understand some basic array principles, and then we will go back to modifying the Paint Program.

Assume we want to create 100 random numbers, all between 0 and 1000. Then we want to find the average of these numbers. If our random number generator is really random, the answer should be something close to 500, so let's write a program to do this and see what result we get. Figure 11.10 shows the necessary code.

```
Dim n[100]
// first create the numbers
for a = 0 to 99
  n[a]=random(1000)
next
// now add up all the numbers
tot = 0
for a = 0 to 99
  tot = tot + n[a]
next
// calculate the average
ave = tot/100
print ave
end
```

Figure 11.10: This code finds the average of 100 random numbers.

The code is commented, so it should be easy to follow. Notice how the variable **tot** was used to keep track of the total of the array. Notice also that it must initially be set to zero. Each time through the loop, the next element is added to the cumulative total. Since there are 100 numbers, we can calculate the average by dividing the total by 100.

Now that you know a little about arrays, let's make a modification to our Paint Program that would be very difficult (if not impossible) to make without the use of arrays.

11.8 Creating Custom Colors

We want to modify the Paint Program so as to allow the user to select any color they want instead of just the 10 colors we have originally provided in the menu.

In order to do this, we will provide a method for the user to substitute the new color for any of the 10 colors shown on the menu. Once this is done, the next time the user selects that box, the new color will be the one chosen for the brush and other color related objects.

In RobotBASIC there are 16 standard colors numbered 0 to 15. This is why if the user chooses box n (0 to 9) we can use the number of the box to represent the color. However, if we are to allow any color from among millions of colors we cannot do this.

If we create an array **Col[ ]** with 10 elements and store the color codes in those elements, then when the user selects box **n** from the menu the color code stored in the element **Col[n]** will be used instead of the number **n** of the box.

Let's see how this works. Suppose the user picks the bottom color box in the menu. The menu system would indicate that box 9 is selected and 9 will be stored in the variable **co** just as before. But, everywhere the program originally used the simple variable **co** to indicate a color, we will substitute **Col[co]**. This will make the program use the color code in the 10th position in the array (remember the count starts at 0 so the number 9 selects the 10th element).

Whenever the user right-clicks the color boxes on the menu we will use the RobotBASIC function `PromptColor()` to give the user a palette of colors to choose from. The user then selects any color from this palette (or even create a new one). Having done this, the function `PromtColor()` will return a number that is the code for the color selected. We will then store this code in the correct element in the **Col[ ]** array.

Another modification we would like is to make the program display instructions to the user upon starting the program.

Let's make these modifications to the subroutines we have written previously to help you see how to implement these concepts. Most subroutines will require only a few changes that will be indicated in **bold**. Also only a portion of the routine will be repeated, just enough to help you see where the changes should be made. Let's look at each subroutine individually (There are no changes to the **MainProgram**).

The new `Print` statements in the modified **Initialization** subroutine (shown if Figure 11.11) display some simple instructions to the user on how to use the program. A `WaitKey` statement lets the user read the instructions until a key is pressed. The variable **k** will hold the value for the key pressed by the user, but since we don't really care what key is pressed, the program just clears the screen and continues as before.

Also notice how the **Col[ ]** array is dimensioned to hold 10 elements and each element is given the appropriate initial value (0 to 9 for the initial colors) with the `for`-loop.

```
Initialization:
  Print "RobotBASIC PAINT PROGRAM"
  Print "    www.RobotBASIC.com"
  Print
  Print "Choose from menu with Mouse"
  Print "Hold down left-but. to draw"
  Print "Rt-click colors to redefine"
  Print "     Press any key"
  WaitKey k
  ClearScr
  co = 0
  br = 2
  bc = 7
  ClearScr 7
  Dim Col[10]
  for i=0 to 9
    Col[i]=i
  next
  gosub DrawMenu
return
```

Figure 11.11: The new **Initialization** routine adds instructions, creates the **Col[ ]** array, and initializes it.

The new **ProcessMenu** subroutine (see Figure 11.12) requires only a few changes. The original if-then statement that allowed for selecting a color has been converted to an if structure that we have not used before. The first portion of this structure checks to see if the left mouse button is pressed, and if so, sets the variable **co** just as before. If the left mouse button was not pressed it uses the elseif to see if the right mouse button was pressed. These decisions could have been made with two if-endif structures, but this is more efficient.

If the right mouse button is pressed, a new function is executed. PromptColor() causes RobotBASIC to display a menu of colors. This allows the user to choose from a wide variety of colors or even create a custom one. Once chosen, this new color is stored into the array so that it will be used in the future (as discussed above). Notice that the

current color of the box selected is passed to
PromptColor(). The number of the box selected is **b/60**
making the current color of that box **Col[b/60]**. This color
will be returned by PromptColor() if the user does not
select a new color. The menu is then redrawn so that the
newly chosen color will show in the appropriate box in the
menu.

```
ProcessMenu:
  ReadMouse a,b,c
  if a>125 or c=0 then return
  if within(a,60,125)
     // process color
     if c=1
        co = b/60
     elseif c=2
        Col[b/60]=PromptColor(Col[b/60])
        gosub DrawMenu
     endif
  else
     if within(b,240,300) then br=2
     if within(b,300,360) then br=6
     if within(b,360,420) then br=12
     if within(b,420,480) then br=26
     if within(b,480,540) then br=32
     if within(b,180,240)
        bc = co
        clearscr Col[bc]
        gosub DrawMenu
     endif
// truncated, the rest is unchanged
```

Figure 11.12: The user can now redefine the colors.

The new **DrawMenu** subroutine (see Figure 11.13) has only
one line changed. When the colors are drawn, the **Col[ ]**
array provides the color code to be used.

```
DrawMenu:
  LineWidth 3
  c=0
  for i=0 to 540 step 60
    Rectangle 1,i,65,i+60,black,white
    Rectangle 65,i,125,i+60,black,Col[c]
    c=c+1
  next
// truncated, the rest is unchanged
```

Figure 11.13: The modified menu allows for selecting millions of colors.

The new **DrawBrush** is shown in Figure 11.14 and the new **Now** routine is shown in Figure 11.15. The rectangles in the FILL and CLEAR options and the currently selected brush are redrawn using the color codes in the **Col[ ]** array.

```
DrawBrush:
  // assumes br defines the brush and
  // co is the color
  // a,b,c are the mouse data
  while c=1
    if a>125
      if br<20
        s=br
        Circle a-s,b-s,a+s,b+s,Col[co],Col[co]
      else
        s=(br-20)
        Circle a-s,b-s,a+s,b+s,Col[co],Col[bc]
      endif
    endif
    ReadMouse a,b,c
  wend
return
```

Figure 11.14: The original **DrawBrush** has been changed to allow the array to specify the colors to be drawn.

```
Now:
  Rectangle 10,150,55,170,Col[co],Col[co]
  Rectangle 10,210,55,230,Col[co],Col[co]
  a=32
  b=577
  s=12
  Circle a-s,b-s,a+s,b+s,white,white
  if br<20
    s=br
    Circle a-s,b-s,a+s,b+s,Col[co],Col[co]
  else
    s=(br-20)
    Circle a-s,b-s,a+s,b+s,Col[co],Col[bc]
  endif
return
```

Figure 11.15: The color codes in the **Col[ ]** array are used to update the menu to current conditions.

11.9 Trying the Updated Program

Make all the changes shown above and run the program. You will see that it now starts by showing some instructions on how to use the program. (As an exercise, you might try making these instructions more helpful). Press any key to clear the screen and continue with the program.

The program seems to respond just like before. If you right-click one of the color boxes on the menu though, you will see a totally new menu appear. This one is provided by the PromptColor() function. It allows you to choose from many colors or even create one of your own. Try choosing some totally new color and verify that it replaces the original color in the selected box. Use the new color to draw on the screen.

11.10 Summary

In this chapter you have learned:

❑ More about the program-design process.

❑ How to create a relatively complex menu.

❑ Some insights into how programs can be more efficient.

❑ How to save and restore the output screen.

❑ How to use millions of colors in RobotBASIC.

❑ How arrays add to the power of programming.

11.11 Exercises

Before moving on to the next chapter, test your knowledge and skill by trying the following exercises. Give each problem your best effort before reviewing the answers given in Appendix A.

1. Even though we made a good effort to prevent the user from drawing on the menu, you will see that the edge of the brush can sometimes protrude into the menu area. This happens because we only made sure the *center* of the brush never entered the menu area. Modify the program so that the user cannot draw on the menu at all.

> **Hint:** Make sure that none of the brush is ever over the menu. Do this by changing the `if` statement in **DrawBrush** that keeps you from drawing on the menu.

2. Research the Help Pages to read about the function `MsgBox()` and see if you can use it to give the instructions for the Paint Program a more professional look.

3. Think about how you would expand the menu or otherwise enable the user to select a color to be used as the background for the open brushes. Currently, the open brushes always use the background color (which is set by default or when the screen is cleared).

4. In the program in Figure 11.10 we set the value of each element in one `for`-loop and then summed the elements in another `for`-loop. Examine the help files and see if you can find two ways to make this program more efficient?

> **Hint:** Setting the values and totaling can be done in the same loop. Also read about the `mAverage()` and the `mSum()` functions.

Chapter 12

Where To Go From Here

RobotBASIC has many powerful commands and functions that were not covered in this introductory text. They allow you to draw buttons, select files, play songs, display pictures, and much, much more. Now that you have a basic understanding of how to program, you should be able to read through the help files and discover many new additions for your programming vocabulary. Hopefully we have been able to motivate you to continue your studies.

You will find a wide variety of example programs at **www.RobotBASIC.com** that can help with more advanced subjects by showing you how commands can be used. You will see, for example, how to create interesting video games with far more features than our cannon program. There are also numerous robot programs that you can examine if you enjoyed programming the simulated robot.

If you find you need more help, especially with robot programming, check out the book *Robot Programmer's Bonanza*, at your local bookstore or read a sample chapter on our web page. You will learn all about the RobotBASIC simulator and even discover that RobotBASIC has many commands that allow you to control real robots too.

Programming is best learned with practice. Hopefully you now find the challenges of programming exciting and rewarding and we hope that you will always enjoy using RobotBASIC for your programming language.

The principles of programming in any language have many similarities. As you become proficient with RobotBASIC, you should find it easy to learn other languages too. So whether you just continue with RobotBASIC or need to transition to other languages for your work or school, we hope this book has increased your skills and knowledge. Always check-in at our web page to download the latest version of RobotBASIC and see all the latest news (such as current Magazine articles utilizing RobotBASIC).

RobotBASIC is one of the easiest languages available for the PC, yet it is one of the most powerful. Hopefully it will continue to fulfill your needs as your programming skills increase.

We are constantly upgrading and improving RobotBASIC, so if you have any suggestions or ideas, please pass them on to us through our web page.

Appendix A

Solutions To Exercises

The solutions for all the exercises in the book will be shown and explained in this Appendix. Remember, these are just *Example* solutions and are not necessarily the only way to solve the exercise.

The solutions for each chapter start on a new page to make them easy to locate.

Solutions: Chapter 1

Solution for challenge in Section 1.8

```
SetColor RED
LineWidth 3
Line 0,0,799,599
SetColor Green
LineWidth 20
Line 799,0,100,400
SetColor Blue
LineWidth 5
Line 400,300,799,300
End
```

Solution for challenge in Section 1.9

The dimension given in Figure 1.6 help you in determining the coordinates (x,y) of the points required to define the rectangle and the triangle.

For the rectangle:
Top left corner   x = 400   y = 300
Bottom right corner x = 700   y = 500
For the triangle:
1st vertex (top left)   x = 100   y = 100
2nd vertex (bottom right) x = 400   y = 200
3rd vertex (bottom left)   x = 100   y = 300

Also as indicated we need the line width to be set to 3. So now we can derive the program as:

```
linewidth 3
rectangle 400,300,700,500,blue
line 100,100,400,200,3,blue
lineto 100,300,3,blue
lineto 100,100,3,blue
```

Solution for challenge in Section 1.10

Remember that the rSpeed command will cause the robot to be slower when it is given a bigger the number and vice versa.

```
rLocate 100,200
rTurn 90
rspeed 220    //make it go slowly
rForward 500
rTurn 180
rspeed 0    //make it go fastest
rForward 500
End
```

Solution for Exercise 1.1

```
rlocate 20,20
rturn 90
rforward 760
rturn 90
rforward 560
rturn 90
rforward 760
rturn 90
rforward 560
```

Solution for Exercise 1.2

To make the robot go diagonally from top left corner to bottom right corner we need to place the robot at position (20,20) then turn the robot to face the bottom right corner then forward the distance required. You could use math (the Pythagorean Theorem) to determine these values, but for now, just experiment to find the required values for the turn direction and the distance. Appropriate values are shown below.

```
rlocate 20,20
rturn 126
distance = 939
rforward distance
rturn 180
rforward distance
```

Solutions: Chapter 2

Solution for Challenge in Section 2.4

The changes to make the program draw squares will have to be done for *each* line in the program. Lots of work! You also have to do some addition to get the correct value for the y-coordinate. The code listed below lets RobotBASIC to do the math.

```
LineWidth 3
Rectangle 100,100,350,100+250
Rectangle 400,100,650,100+250
Rectangle 400,350,650,350+250
Rectangle 100,350,350,350+250
End
```

Solution for Challenge in Section 2.7

See solution for Exercise 2.5 below.

Solution for Exercise 2.1

```
LineWidth 3
Rectangle 100,100,350,200,red,red
Rectangle 400,100,650,200,blue,blue
Rectangle 400,350,650,450,yellow,yellow
Rectangle 100,350,350,450,brown,brown
End
```

Solution for Exercise 2.2

```
width = 250
height = 100
x = 100
y = 100
linewidth 5
Rectangle x,y,x+width,y+height
x = 400
linewidth 8
Rectangle x,y,x+width,y+height
y = 350
linewidth 3
Rectangle x,y,x+width,y+height
x = 100
linewidth 15
Rectangle x,y,x+width,y+height
End
```

Solution for Exercise 2.3

In this exercise the idea is for you to realize the advantage of having variables instead of numbers. Using variables you can just change one line of code to change many places in the program wherever the variable is being used. So notice how much easier it was to do the modification in the second version than in the first version.

```
//had to change every line and figure out
//the value by adding
LineWidth 3
Rectangle 100,100,200,200
Rectangle 400,100,500,200
Rectangle 400,350,500,450
Rectangle 100,350,200,450
End
```

Now for the easy way.

```
//easy just one change
LineWidth 3
width = 100    //just here
height = 100
x = 100
y = 100
Rectangle x,y,x+width,y+height
x = 400
Rectangle x,y,x+width,y+height
y = 350
Rectangle x,y,x+width,y+height
x = 100
Rectangle x,y,x+width,y+height
End
```

Solution for Exercise 2.4

```
//need to get X,Y
Print "This program will draw four
rectangles."
Print "It will allow you to specify the
width and height."
Print "it will also allow you to specify
the x,y position"
print "    of the top left corner of the
last drawn rectangle"
Input "Enter Width", width
Input "Enter Height", height
Input "Enter X value",X   //capital X
Input "Enter Y value",Y   //capital Y
x = 100
y = 100
Rectangle x,y,x+width,y+height
x = 400
Rectangle x,y,x+width,y+height
y = 350
Rectangle x,y,x+width,y+height
x = 100
//notice using Capital X and Y
Rectangle X,Y,X+width,Y+height
End
```

Solution for Exercise 2.5

Here is a suggested path. Notice how the code lets
RobotBASIC do the math work. The number 20 is used to
make sure the robot stays 20 pixels away from the walls.
This is because the robot has a radius of 20 pixels. This will
ensure the robot does not crash into the walls.

```
LineWidth 3
Rectangle 200,400,500,550
Circle 200,200,400,300
Line 400,100,700,500
rLocate 350,350
// Enter your code here
  rturn -90
  rforward 200
  rturn 90
  rforward 350-20
  rturn 90
  rforward 800-20-150
End
```

Solutions: Chapter 3

Solution for Exercise 3.1

```
LineWidth 3
size = 50
for a = 1 to 10   //change the 10 to 30
                  //for the next part
   x = Random(700)
   y = Random(500)
   Rectangle x,y,x+2*size,y+size
  Delay 100
next
End
```

Solution for Exercise 3.2

```
LineWidth 3
size = 50
for a = 1 to 20
   x = Random(700)
   y = Random(500)
   Rectangle x,y,x+size,y+2*size //changed here
   Delay 100
next
End
```

Solution for Exercise 3.3

```
LineWidth 3
size = 50
for a = 1 to 20
   x = Random(700)
   y = Random(500)
   SetColor Random(15)
   Rectangle x,y,x+2*size,y+size
   Delay 100
next
End
```

Solution for Exercise 3.4

The given formula creates a random number between 50 and 50+150 (i.e. 200), since the function `Random(150)` will give a random number between 0 and 150.

```
LineWidth 3
for a = 1 to 20
   x = Random(700)
   y = Random(500)
   size = Random(150)+50
   Rectangle x,y,x+2*size,y+size
   Delay 100
next
End
```

Solutions: Chapter 4

Solution for Exercise 4.2

We need to change the program so that it tests the x-coordinate (right and left not up and down).

```
LineWidth 3
size = 50
for c = 1 to 20
    x = random(700)
    y = random(500)
    if x<400    //changed here
        Circle x,y,x+2*size,y+size,green,green
    else
        Rectangle x,y,x+size,y+size,red,red
    endif
    Delay 100
next
end
```

Solution for Exercise 4.3

```
LineWidth 3
for c = 1 to 20
    x = random(700)
    y = random(500)
    size = 10+random(100)
    if y<300
        Circle x,y,x+2*size,y+size
    else
        Rectangle x,y,x+size,y+size
    endif
    Delay 100
next
end
```

Solution for Exercise 4.4

This exercise requires a few changes, see the comments in the program code.

```
LineWidth 3
size = 50
for c = 1 to 20
    x = random(700)
    y = random(500)
    if y<300
        if x<400
            SetColor Blue
            rectangle x,y,x+2*size,y+size
            //new line
        else
            SetColor Red
            Circle x,y,x+2*size,y+size
            //new line
        endif
    else
        if x<400
            SetColor Green
            Circle x,y,x+size,y+size
            //new line
        else
            SetColor Black
            Rectangle x,y,x+size,y+size
            //new line
        endif
    endif
    Delay 100
next
end
```

Solutions: Chapter 5

Solution for Exercise 5.1

The statement `SetColor Red` causes all future drawing to be in that color. So we need to change the color again after drawing all the squares on the top of the screen so that any new drawing will be black. See where that is done in the code below.

```
xyString 15,20,"small"
Rectangle 730,0,799,50
xyString 740,20,"large"
// setup default size
size = 50
xyString 350,20,"LARGE"
SetColor Black   // add this line
while True
    //rest of the program is the same
```

Solution for Exercise 5.2

```
LineWidth 3
// Draw two rectangles
// label them small and large
SetColor Red
Rectangle 0,0,70,50
xyString 15,20,"small"
//---draw box and label it
Rectangle 90,0,160,50
xyString 102,20,"medium"
Rectangle 730,0,799,50
xyString 740,20,"large"
// setup default size
size = 50
xyString 350,20,"LARGE"
while True
    ReadMouse x,y,b
    // see if mouse is at top of screen
    // with a button pressed
    if Within(y,0,50) and (b=1 or b=2)
        if Within(x,90,160)
            //---allow for selecting
            //    and setting medium size
            size = 30
            xyString 350,20,"MEDIUM"
        endif
        //----rest of program is as before
```

Solution for Exercise 5.3

```
// setup default size
size = 50
xyString 350,20,"LARGE"
while True
    if Within(y,0,50) and (b=1 or b=2)
        //code here is not changed
        //and is not shown for brevity
    else
        // not at top so check for drawing
        if b=1
            //new code
            Line x,y,x,y+size
            s = size/2
            Line x-s,y+s,x+s,y+s
        endif
        if b=2 then Circle x,y,x+size,y+size
    endif
wend
end
```

Solutions: Chapter 6

Solution for Exercise 6.3

The function `rFeel()` uses sensors numbered similarly to `rBumper()`. The difference is `rFeel()` does not have to bump into the object to detect it (it simulates infrared light reflecting off the object). Therefore,

just change the line
```
bump = rBumper
```
to the line
```
bump = rFeel()
```

Solution for Exercise 6.4

The `rInvisible` command has many options, but you can change the color of the trail left by the robot by simply specifying the color you want after the `rInvisible` command.

Solutions: Chapter 7

Solution for Exercise 7.2

The program in Figure 6.4 is converted to a modular program using the ideas in Chapter 6.

```
MainProgram:
  GoSub Initialize
  GoSub MoveRobot
End
Initialize:
    // create the robot near the
    // center of the screen
    size = 50
    LineWidth 3
    rLocate 400,300
    rTurn 20
Return
CheckMouse:
    // draw an object if mouse is clicked
    ReadMouse x,y,b
    if b=1 then Rectangle x,y,x+size,y+size
    if b=2 then Circle x,y,x+size,y+size
Return
MoveRobot:
    while True
        // move forward till bumped
        while rBumper()=0
            rForward 1
            GoSub CheckMouse
        wend
        bump = rBumper()
        // back up one pixel
        if bump <> 1 then rForward -1
        // now turn away
        Ta = 0
        if bump = 2 or bump = 6 then Ta = -130
        if bump = 8 or bump = 12 then Ta = 130
        if bump=4 or bump=14 then Ta= 140+random(80)
        rTurn Ta
    wend
Return
```

Solutions: Chapter 8

Solution for Exercise 8.1

We want the ball to move down every time it moves to the right. The easiest way to see this happen is to simply replace all the **y**'s with **x**'s.

```
// y=300   this line is no longer needed
size=20
LineWidth 3
for x = 1 to 800
   circle x,x,x+size,x+size,blue,red
   delay 10
   circle x,x,x+size,x+size,white,white
next
end
```

Solution for Exercise 8.2

The order of drawing affects which part over-laps the other. The bottom half of the cannon must overlap the circle and the circle must overlap the barrel. Try changing the order to see the results.

```
GoSub DrawCannon
end
DrawCannon:
   Line 50,550,100,500,20,brown
   Circle 0,500,100,600,Blue,Blue
   Rectangle 0,550,100,600,red,red
   Flip
Return
```

Solution for Exercise 8.3

Only the routines where there is a change will be listed below.

```
Initialization:
  xs=150
  ys=530
  dx=1
  dy=1
  size=10
  //the rest is the same as before and
  //is not listed for brevity
Return
DrawCannon:
  Circle 0,500,100,600,Blue,Blue
  Rectangle 0,550,100,600,Blue,Blue
  Line 50,530,120,530,20,Blue
  Flip
Return
MoveBall:
  //assumes the following
  // size is the size of the ball
  // xs,ys is the starting point
  // dx and dy are the increments
  // MB and S are temporary variables
  // incX and incY are temporary variables
  // x and y are temporary variables
  x = xs
  y = ys
  S=size/2
  PlayWav "FireCannon"
  gosub Fire
  while x<800 and y>0
      circle x-S,y-S,x+S,y+S,Black,Black
      flip
      delay 10
      circle x-S,y-S,x+S,y+S,White,White
      incX=dx*power/20.0
      incY=-dy*power/20.0
      if incX<1 then incX=1
      if incY>-1 then incY=-1
      x=x+incX
      //y=y+incY   notice the line is removed
  wend
  repeat
    ReadMouse a,b,c
  until c=0
  Flip
Return
```

Solutions: Chapter 9

Solution for Exercise 9.1

You must reverse the wind when the ball reaches the left or right screen limits (just like we did for the vertical movement).

```
x = 30    // horizontal position of the ball
y = 300   // vertical position of the ball
          // initialized to the starting position
s = 0     // speed of ball initialized to zero
g = .1    // our guess at our gravity factor
El = 1    //elasticity factor
wind = 1 //wind speed
flip on
while true
   x = x+wind
   if not within(x,0,780) //reached left or right
     wind = -wind          //reverse wind
     if x<0 then x=0    //no move beyond limits
     if x>780 then x=780
   endif
   circle x,y,x+20,y+20,red,black // draw ball
   flip
   circle x,y,x+20,y+20,white,white // erase ball
   y = y+s // calculate the new ball position
   s = s+g // calculate the new speed
   // now reverse the ball if it hits the ground
   // by making the speed negative
   if y>580
      y=581     //don't let it go too far
      s= -s*El //reverse and slow down
   endif
wend
end
```

Solutions: Chapter 10

Solution for challenge in Section 10.3

The reason we use the -3 to +60 range is due to the way the tank is drawn using the `DrawShape` command. If you analyze how the letters in the variable **Tank** make the tank be drawn from the reference coordinate **Tx,599** and allow for the scale you will see that the tank will occupy the area **Tx-5** to **Tx+45** and allowing for the ball size and the fact the tank is drawn with a thick line then -3 to +60 is a good bound for the ball to be in to be redeemed to have hit the tank.

Solution for Exercise 10.3

Here is an example of making the tank bigger. Just the modified routines are shown. Try values of 3 and 20 for TS. Notice the size of the explosion will change too (see the code changes on the next page).

```
InitTank:
  TS = 10 // the new scale for the tank
  tank = "quwrrwqsrrsrrsdallllllll"
  Tx = 200+Random(550)
  DrawShape tank,Tx,599,TS
  gosub MoveTank
return

MoveTank:
  // Tx is the current tank location
  // move it a random distance but never less
  // than 200 nor more than 750
  // now choose a new location
  tx = 200+Random(550)
  for t = Tx to tx
     DrawShape tank,t,599,TS
     flip
     DrawShape tank,t,599,TS,-1
  next
  Tx = tx
  DrawShape tank,Tx,599,TS
  flip
return

Explosion:
  PlayWav "Explode"
  for t = 5 to TS*10 step 2
     circle x-t,590-t,x+t,590+t,red,random(16)
     flip
     delay 20
  next
  for t = TS*10 to 3 step -2
     circle x-t,590-t,x+t,590+t,white,gray
     flip
  next
return

MoveBall:
  // many lines omitted here
  Flip
  if within(x,Tx-3,Tx+TS*10) // changes range of hit
     hit = true
     gosub Explosion
  endif
  NumShots = NumShots+1
Return
```

Solutions: Chapter 11

Solution for challenge in Section 11.3

The reason the **Now** subroutine should be called every time a new color or brush is selected is so that the menu box, which shows the type and color of the current brush, will be displaying the correct information.

Solution for challenge in Section 11.4

The reason the **DrawMenu** routine is called is because the ReadScreen command will overwrite the current menu (the ENTIRE screen is saved, not just the drawing area) and thus we need to redraw the menu so that the correct menu (current colors and so on) is displayed.

Solution for Exercise 11.1

Only the modified portion of the routine is given.

```
DrawBrush:
  // assumes br defines the brush and
  // co is the color
  // a,b,c are the mouse data
  if br>20
     radius = br-20
  else
     radius = br
  endif
  while c=1
    if a>125+radius
      if br<20
// no more changes needed
```

Solution for Exercise 11.2

```
Initialization:
  Dim IM[10]
  IM[0] = "Paint Program"
  IM[1] = "RobotBASIC PAINT PROGRAM"
  IM[2] = "  www.RobotBASIC.com"
  IM[3] = ""
  IM[4] = "Choose from menu with Mouse"
  IM[5] = "Hold down left-button to draw"
  IM[6] = "Right-click colors to redefine"
  n = MsgBox(IM)
  ClearScr
  // rest is the same and not listed
return
```

Solution for Exercise 11.3

The method chosen is as follows: If you right-click either of the open brushes, that brush will be chosen and the background color will be set to the current color. Just select a new current color and you will see the new brush at the bottom of the menu (See the routine on the next page)

```
ProcessMenu:
  ReadMouse a,b,c
  if a>125 or c=0 then return
  if within(a,60,125)
    // process color
    if c=1
      co = b/60
    elseif c=2
      Col[b/60]=PromptColor()
      gosub DrawMenu
    endif
  else
    if c=1
    // other menu item
      if within(b,240,300) then br=2
      if within(b,300,360) then br=6
      if within(b,360,420) then br=12
      if within(b,420,480) then br=26
      if within(b,480,540) then br=32
      if within(b,180,240)
        bc = co
        clearscr bc
        gosub DrawMenu
      endif
      if within(b,120,180)
        SetCursor -3
        repeat
          ReadMouse a,b,c
        until c=0
        repeat
          ReadMouse a,b,c
        until c=1
        if a>125 then FloodFill a,b,Col[co]
        SetCursor
      endif
      if within(b,0,60)
        Input "OPENING: Enter a File Name",filename
        if filename<>"" then ReadScr(filename)
        gosub DrawMenu
      endif
      if within(b,60,120)
        Input "SAVING: Enter a File Name",filename
        WriteScr(filename)
      endif
    elseif c=2
      // an open brush was right-clicked
      if within(b,420,540)
        // set the new background color
        bc = co
        // then set the new brush style
        if within(b,420,480)
          br=26
        else
          br=32
        endif
        gosub DrawMenu
      endif
    endif
  endif
  gosub Now
return
```

Solution for Exercise 11.4

Here are two new versions of the program in Figure 11.10 that do the same thing but are much shorter and would take much less time to execute. The second version is a lot faster than the first one. This is a demonstration of how RobotBASIC has many commands and functions that can make your programs a lot more efficient because they can replace code that you normally would write yourself.

The time saving would not be noticeable for a small number of elements, but when the elements become large (e.g. 10,000 elements) then the difference in time can be very noticeable. Try it! If you need a stopwatch look up the function `Timer()`.

```
Dim n[100]
//create the numbers and sum them up
tot = 0
for a = 0 to 99
  n[a]=random(1000)
  tot = tot+n[a] //calculate the total
next
// calculate the average
ave = tot/100
print tot;ave
end
```

```
Dim n[100]
// first create the numbers
for a = 0 to 99
  n[a]=random(1000)
next
print mSum(n); mAverage(n)
end
```

Index

INDEX (continued)

19532092R00093

Made in the USA
Lexington, KY
22 December 2012